CW00502111

16(

Essential Italian

Phrases

Easy to Intermediate

Pocket Size Phrase Book for Travel

By

Fluency Pro

Disclaimer

Without the publisher's prior written consent, no portion of this publication may be reproduced, stored in a retrieval system, or transmitted in any form or by any means, electronic, mechanical, photocopying, recording, scanning, or otherwise, except as permitted under Sections 107 or 108 of the United States Copyright Act of 1976. Although every precaution has been taken in preparing this book, the publisher is not liable for any mistakes, omissions, or damages resulting from the use of the material included within. This book is intended solely for entertainment and educational purposes. The opinions presented are those of the author alone and should not be construed as professional advice or directives. The reader's activities are his or her own responsibility. The author and publisher take no responsibility or liability for the purchaser or reader of these contents. The reader is responsible for his or her own usage of any products or techniques referenced in this publication.

1600+ Essential Italian Phrases
First Edition: March 16, 2023
Copyright © 2023 Caliber Brands Inc.
Cover images licensed through Shutterstock.

Table of Contents

INTRODUCTION 5

ORDERING FOOD 9

BUYING TRAIN TICKETS 13

BUYING AIRLINE TICKETS 18

BEING IN AN EMERGENCY SITUATION 23

ASKING FOR TECH SUPPORT 28

CASUAL CONVERSATION AND SMALL TALK 33

BEING ON A DATE 38

SHOPPING AT A CLOTHING STORE 43

PAYING FOR ITEMS 46

SIMPLE ANSWERS TO THE MOST COMMON QUESTIONS ... 51

ASKING FOR AND GIVING DIRECTIONS 56

COMMON BUSINESS STATEMENTS AND QUESTIONS 61

STAYING AT A HOTEL AND BOOKING A ROOM 67

THE WEATHER 72

WORKING OUT AT A GYM 77

TALKING TO A PHYSICIAN 82

MAKING A MEDICAL APPOINTMENT 87

TALKING TO A DENTIST 93

COMMON GREETINGS 98

BANKING 103

COMMON TRAVELER QUESTIONS 108

COMMON RESPONSES TO QUESTIONS 113

PETS 118

COLORS 122

NUMBERS 126

HANDLING A RUDE PERSON 128

BEING POLITE 135

TALKING ABOUT FAMILY 140

MAKING SUGGESTIONS 145

EXPRESSING OPINIONS... 147

GIVING AND ASKING FOR ADVICE................................... 149

TALKING ABOUT LIKES AND DISLIKES............................. 154

EXPRESSING AGREEMENT AND DISAGREEMENT 159

MAKING EXCUSES... 164

ASKING AND GIVING PERMISSION................................... 169

BUSINESS NEGOTIATION 174

EXPRESSING GRATITUDE AND APOLOGIES...................... 179

GIVING AND RECEIVING COMPLIMENTS 184

MAKING PHONE CALLS 189

DESCRIBING FEELINGS AND EMOTIONS 194

DISCUSSING HEALTH AND WELL-BEING 199

DESCRIBING JOBS AND PROFESSIONS............................. 203

GIVING AND RECEIVING INSTRUCTIONS 208

INTRODUCTION

Welcome! This book provides important terms for communicating with locals and completing daily tasks, such as buying food and requesting directions, when traveling in Italy.

Understanding native phrases and pronunciation when traveling to Italy is essential for several reasons. Firstly, it enables effective communication with locals, allowing you to ask for directions, order food, and express your needs and desires. Secondly, language is an essential part of culture, and by learning native phrases and pronunciation, you can gain a deeper understanding of Italian culture and its people. Additionally, attempting to speak Italian shows that you respect the culture and are making an effort to engage with it, which is likely to be appreciated by locals.

Moreover, understanding basic phrases such as "help" or "emergency" can be crucial in times of need, particularly if you find yourself in a situation where you need to communicate with emergency services or ask for assistance. Finally, knowing the native phrases and pronunciation can also enhance your overall travel experience by allowing you to engage more fully with the local culture and people, and possibly even make new friends.

A phrase book can be an essential tool when traveling to Italy, as it provides you with essential phrases that can help you communicate effectively, order food, ask for directions, and understand the local culture. It can also assist you in case of an emergency by providing phrases to ask for help or medical assistance. Additionally, a phrase book can help you gain a better understanding of Italian culture and its people by providing idioms, proverbs, and other expressions that reflect the local way of life.

Overall, having a basic understanding of Italian language and pronunciation can significantly enhance your travel experience in Italy, making it easier, safer, and more enjoyable.

How This Book Is Organized

In this book, you will find over 1600 common Italian phrases organized by usage or situation.

Every entry has the original English phrase, the Italian translation, and a phonetic description in a standard format. A phonetic transcription is provided so that readers can compare the written Italian words they encounter with the sounds they are already familiar with. A dash separates each syllable in every transcription. Several spaces separate the words. Capitalized syllables are stressed, but lowercase ones are not.

Vowels

Italian vowels are pronounced differently than in English. In Italian, there are five vowel sounds: A, E, I, O, and U. Here's a brief guide on how each vowel is pronounced:

- A: The "A" sound in Italian is similar to the "A" sound in the English word "car," but it is more open and pronounced with the mouth wider.

- E: The "E" sound in Italian is pronounced like the "E" sound in the English word "bed," but it is crisper and shorter.

- I: The "I" sound in Italian is similar to the "I" sound in the English word "meet," but it is shorter and less pronounced.

- O: The "O" sound in Italian is similar to the "O" sound in the English word "boat," but it is shorter and pronounced with the lips more rounded.

- U: The "U" sound in Italian is similar to the "U" sound in the English word "rule," but it is shorter and pronounced with the lips more rounded.

In addition to these basic vowel sounds, Italian also has diphthongs, which are two vowels pronounced together as a single sound. Some common diphthongs in Italian include "ai," "ei," "oi," and "ui."

Consonants

Italian consonants are generally pronounced similarly to their English counterparts, but there are some differences in pronunciation that are important to note. Here's a brief guide on how each consonant is pronounced in Italian:

- B: The "B" sound in Italian is pronounced similarly to English, but it is more explosive and pronounced with the lips pressed together more firmly.
- C: The "C" sound in Italian can be pronounced differently depending on the vowel that follows it. Before "A," "O," or "U," it is pronounced like the "K" sound in English, but before "E" or "I," it is pronounced like the "CH" sound in the English word "church."
- D: The "D" sound in Italian is pronounced similarly to English, but it is more explosive and pronounced with the tongue pressed against the upper teeth.
- F: The "F" sound in Italian is pronounced similarly to English, but it is softer and less pronounced.
- G: The "G" sound in Italian, like "C," can be pronounced differently depending on the vowel that follows it. Before "A," "O," or "U," it is pronounced like the "G" sound in the English word "go," but before "E" or "I," it is pronounced like the "J" sound in the English word "jump."
- L: The "L" sound in Italian is pronounced similarly to English, but it is more pronounced when it appears in the middle of a word.
- M: The "M" sound in Italian is pronounced similarly to English.
- N: The "N" sound in Italian is pronounced similarly to English.
- P: The "P" sound in Italian is pronounced similarly to English, but it is more explosive and pronounced with the lips pressed together more firmly.
- R: The "R" sound in Italian is pronounced differently than in English. It is pronounced with a single tap of the tongue against the roof of the mouth, rather than with the tongue trilling or vibrating as in many English dialects.

- S: The "S" sound in Italian is pronounced similarly to English, but it is more pronounced and sharper.
- T: The "T" sound in Italian is pronounced similarly to English, but it is more explosive and pronounced with the tongue pressed against the upper teeth.

Overall, learning the correct pronunciation of Italian consonants is essential for speaking Italian fluently and being understood by native speakers.

Stressors and Intonation

Stress and intonation are important components of spoken Italian that can significantly affect the meaning of a word or a sentence. In Italian, stress is placed on the second-to-last syllable of a word, which makes it predictable unlike English where stress can fall on any syllable. It is important to pay attention to the stress of a word in Italian because changing the stress can change the meaning of the word. In addition to stress, Italian also uses a lot of intonation to convey meaning.

An inquiring tone is indicated by an upward rise in intonation, while a declarative tone is indicated by a downward fall in intonation. Moreover, Italian speakers use intonation to emphasize certain words or phrases for emphasis or to convey emotion. Understanding the use of stress and intonation in Italian is essential for speaking Italian fluently and being understood by native speakers. It is recommended to practice these elements of spoken Italian with a native speaker or with language learning tools to perfect your pronunciation and delivery.

ORDERING FOOD

Hi, can we see the menu, please?
Ciao, possiamoP vedere il menu, per favore?
(chow, po-ssee-AH-moh veh-DEH-reh eel MEH-nu, per FA-voh-reh)

What's your most popular dish?
Qual è il piatto più popolare?
(kwahl eh eel pee-AH-tto pew PO-poh-lah-reh)

What do you recommend?
Cosa mi consigilia?
(koh-sah mee kohn-SEEL-yah)

Can I get a glass of water, please?
Posso avere un bicchiere d'acqua, per favore?
(POHs-soh ah-VEH-reh oon bee-KYEH-reh DAH-kwah, per FA-voh-reh)

I'd like to order the steak, please.
Vorrei ordinare la bistecca, per favore.
(vor-RAY or-dee-NAH-reh lah bee-STEHK-kah, per FA-voh-reh)

Can I have a side salad with that?
Posso avere un'insalata come contorno?
(POHs-soh ah-VEH-reh oon-een-sah-LAH-tah KO-meh kohn-TOR-noh)

Do you have any vegetarian options?
Avete opzioni vegetariane?
(ah-VEH-teh ohp-TZYO-nee veh-geh-tah-RYAH-neh)

How spicy is the curry?
Quanto è piccante il curry?
(KWAN-toh eh pee-KAHN-teh eel KOO-ree)

Can I substitute the fries for a baked potato?
Posso sostituire le patatine fritte con una patata al forno?
(POHs-soh sohs-TOO-ee-reh leh pah-tah-TEE-neh FREET-teh kohn OO-nah pah-TAH-tah al FOR-noh)

I'll have a beer, please.
Prendo una birra, per favore.
(PREN-doh OO-nah BEER-rah, per FA-voh-reh)

Do you have any specials today?
Avete delle specialità oggi?
(ah-VEH-teh DEHL-leh speh-chee-ah-LEE-tah OH-jee)

Can we get a bread basket to start?
Possiamo avere un cestino di pane per iniziare?
(POHs-soh ah-VEH-reh oon cheh-STEE-noh dee PAH-neh per in-ee-TSYAH-reh)

Can we split the bill?
Possiamo dividere il conto?
(POHs-soh-moh dee-VEE-deh-reh eel KON-toh)

Can I pay with a credit card?
Posso pagare con la carta di credito?
(POHs-soh pah-GAH-reh kohn lah KAR-tah dee kre-DEE-toh)

Can I have the bill, please?
Il conto, per favore.
(eel KON-toh, per FA-voh-reh)

How much is it altogether?
Quanto costa in totale?
(KWAN-toh KO-stah een toh-TAH-leh)

Excuse me, I think there's a mistake on the bill.
Mi scusi, penso che ci sia un errore sul conto.
(mee SKOO-zee, PEN-soh kee chee SEE-ah oon er-RO-reh sool KON-toh)

Keep the change.
Tenga il resto.
(TEN-gah eel REH-stoh)

Can you bring us more bread, please?
Ci porta ancora del pane, per favore?
(chee POR-tah an-KOR-rah del PAH-neh, per FA-voh-reh)

Is there a service charge?
C'è il servizio incluso?
(cheh eel sehr-VEE-tzyoh een-CLOO-soh)

I'm allergic to nuts.
Sono allergico alle noci.
(SO-noh al-LEHR-jee-koh AH-leh NO-chee)

This is delicious!
e delizioso!
(eh deh-lee-TSYOH-zoh)

Can we have the check, please?
Possiamo avere il conto, per favore?
(POHs-soh-moh ah-VEH-reh eel KON-toh, per FA-voh-reh)

Is there a minimum order for delivery?
C'è un ordine minimo per la consegna?
(cheh oon or-DEE-neh MEE-nee-moh per lah kohn-SEH-nyah)

Can we split the appetizer?
Possiamo dividere l'antipasto?
(POHs-soh-moh dee-VEE-deh-reh lan-tee-PAH-stoh)

I'd like my steak well-done, please.
Vorrei la mia bistecca ben cotta, per favore.
(vor-RAY lah MEE-ah bee-STEHK-kah ben KOT-tah, per FA-voh-reh)

Can we sit outside?
Possiamo sederci fuori?
(POHs-soh-moh seh-DEHR-chee FWOH-ree)

Can I have the dressing on the side?
Posso avere il condimento a parte?
(POHs-soh ah-VEH-reh eel kon-dee-MEN-toh ah PAR-teh)

Is there a children's menu?
C'è un menu per bambini?
(cheh oon MEH-nu per bahm-BEE-nee)

Can we have separate checks?
Possiamo avere conti separati?
(POHs-soh-moh ah-VEH-reh KON-tee seh-pah-RAH-tee)

I'll have the soup of the day, please.
Prendo la zuppa del giorno, per favore.
(PREN-doh lah ZOOP-pah del JOR-noh, per FA-voh-reh)

Can I have a to-go box?
Posso avere un contenitore da asporto?
(POHs-soh ah-VEH-reh oon kohn-teh-nee-TOH-reh dah ah-SPOR-toh)

Can you bring the check, please?
Ci porta il conto, per favore?
(chee POR-tah eel KON-toh, per FA-voh-reh)

Do you accept credit cards?
Accettate le carte di credito?
(ah-chet-TAH-teh leh KAR-teh dee kreh-DEE-toh)

I'm sorry, but I didn't order this.
Mi scusi, ma non ho ordinato questo.
(mee SKOO-zee, mah non oh or-dee-NAH-toh KWEH-stoh)

Can you recommend a dish?
Può consigliarci un piatto?
(pwò kon-see-LYAR-chee oon PYAH-ttoh)

Can we see the dessert menu?
Possiamo vedere il menu dei dolci?
(POHs-soh-moh veh-DEH-reh eel MEH-nu day DOHL-chee)

The food was excellent!
Il cibo era eccellente!
(eel CHEE-boh EH-rah eh-tchel-LEN-teh)

May I have a glass of water, please?
Posso avere un bicchiere d'acqua, per favore?
(POHs-soh ah-VEH-reh oon bee-KYEH-reh DAH-kwah, per FA-voh-reh)

BUYING TRAIN TICKETS

Hello, can I buy a ticket please?
Ciao, posso comprare un biglietto per favore?
(chow, PO-so kom-PRA-re oon beel-YET-to pair fa-VO-re)

I'd like to purchase a ticket.
Vorrei acquistare un biglietto.
(vo-REY ak-kwes-TA-re oon beel-YET-to)

What is the fare for a one-way ticket to [destination]?
Quanto costa un biglietto di sola andata per [destination]?
(KWAN-to KOS-ta oon beel-YET-to dee SO-la an-DA-ta pair [ ])

How much does a round-trip ticket to [destination] cost?
Quanto costa un biglietto di andata e ritorno per [destination]?
(KWAN-to KOS-ta oon beel-YET-to dee an-DA-ta ey re-TOR-no pair [ ])

Can I get a discount on my ticket?
Posso avere uno sconto sul mio biglietto?
(PO-so a-VEY-re o-no SCON-to sul MIO beel-YET-to)

Do you offer student discounts?
Offrite sconti per gli studenti?
(of-FREE-te SCON-tee pair ly stu-DEN-tee)

Are there any promotional fares available?
Ci sono tariffe promozionali disponibili?
(che SO-no ta-REE-fe pro-mo-tzyo-NA-lee dis-po-NI-bi-lee)

How much is a first-class ticket?
Quanto costa un biglietto di prima classe?
(KWAN-to KOS-ta oon beel-YET-to dee PREE-ma KLAS-se)

Can I book a specific seat?
Posso prenotare un posto specifico?
(PO-so pre-no-TA-re oon PO-sto spe-see-FIG-ko)

Is there a train leaving for [destination] soon?
C'è un treno che parte presto per [destination]?
(che oon TRE-no key PAR-tey PRES-to pair [ ])

What is the next available train to [destination]?
Qual è il prossimo treno disponibile per [destination]?
(kwal ey il PROS-si-mo TRE-no dis-po-NI-bi-lee pair [ ])

Can I reserve a seat on the next train to [destination]?
Posso prenotare un posto sul prossimo treno per [destination]?
(PO-so pre-no-TA-re oon PO-sto sul PROS-si-mo TRE-no pair [ ])

How long is the journey to [destination]?
Quanto dura il viaggio per [destination]?
(KWAN-to DOO-ra il vy-AG-gyo pair [ ])

Is there a direct train to [destination]?
C'è un treno diretto per [destination]?
(che oon TRE-no dee-REK-to pair [ ])

Do I need to transfer trains to get to [destination]?
Devo cambiare treno per arrivare a [destination]?
(DE-vo kam-BYA-re TRE-no pair ar-REE-var-rey a [ ])

How many stops are there between here and [destination]?
Quante fermate ci sono tra qui e [destination]?
(KWAN-te fer-MA-te che SO-no tra kwey ey [ ])

Can I buy a ticket for a later train?
Posso comprare un big lietto per un treno successivo?
(PO-so kom-PRA-re oon beel-YET-to pair oon TRE-no suc-CES-si-vo)

Can I exchange my ticket for a different time or date?
Posso cambiare il mio biglietto per un'altra ora o data?
(PO-so kam-BYA-re il MIO beel-YET-to pair oon'al-tra O-ra o DA-ta)

What time does the train leave?
A che ora parte il treno?
(a key O-ra PAR-tey il TRE-no)

What time does the train arrive?
A che ora arriva il treno?
(a key O-ra ar-REE-va il TRE-no)

Can I get a timetable?
Posso avere un orario dei treni?
(PO-so a-VEY-re oon o-RA-ry-o dei TRE-nee)

Can I pay with a credit card?
Posso pagare con una carta di credito?
(PO-so pa-GA-rey kon oon KA-rrta dee kre-DI-to)

Can I pay with cash?
Posso pagare in contanti?
(PO-so pa-GA-rey in kon-TAN-tee)

Can I buy a ticket online?
Posso comprare un biglietto online?
(PO-so kom-PRA-re oon beel-YET-to on-LINE)

Where is the ticket counter?
Dov'è lo sportello per i biglietti?
(do-VEY lo spor-TEL-lo pair ee beel-YET-tee)

Can I pick up my tickets at the station?
Posso ritirare i miei biglietti alla stazione?
(PO-so ree-tee-RA-rey ee MIE-ee beel-YET-tee al-la sta-TZYON-ey)

Do I need to show ID to buy a ticket?
Devo mostrare un documento d'identità per comprare un biglietto?
(DE-vo mo-STRAR-ey oon do-KU-men-to dee-den-TEE-ta pair kom-PRA-re oon beel-YET-to)

Can I buy a ticket for someone else?
Posso comprare un biglietto per qualcun altro?
(PO-so kom-PRA-re oon beel-YET-to pair KWAHL-kun AL-tro)

Can I get a refund on my ticket?
Posso avere un rimborso sul mio biglietto?
(PO-so a-VEY-re oon rim-BOR-so sul MIO beel-YET-to)

Do I need to validate my ticket before boarding the train?
Devo convalidare il mio biglietto prima di salire sul treno?
(DE-vo kon-va-lee-DA-rey il MIO beel-YET-to PREE-ma dee sa-LEE-rey sul TRE-no)

Where do I validate my ticket?
Dove posso convalidare il mio biglietto?
(DO-vey PO-so kon-va-lee-DA-rey il MIO beel-YET-to)

Can I bring luggage on the train?
Posso portare bagagli sul treno?
(PO-so por-TA-rey ba-GA-lee sul TRE-no)

Is there a luggage storage at the station?
C'è un deposito bagagli alla stazione?
(che ey oon de-po-ZEE-to ba-GA-lee al-la sta-TZYON-ey)

Can I bring a pet on the train?
Posso portare un animale domestico sul treno?
(PO-so por-TA-rey oon a-ni-MA-le do-MES-ti-ko sul TRE-no)

Are there any discounts available?
Ci sono sconti disponibili?
(che SO-no SKON-tee dis-po-NEE-bi-lee)

How much does a ticket cost?
Quanto costa un biglietto?
(KWAN-to KOS-ta oon beel-YET-to)

Is there a first class option?
C'è un'opzione di prima classe?
(che ey oon op-TZY-o-ney dee PREE-ma KLAS-se)

Is there a second class option?
C'è un'opzione di seconda classe?
(che ey oon op-TZY-o-ney dee se-KON-da KLAS-se)

Can I reserve a seat?
Posso prenotare un posto a sedere?
(PO-so pre-no-TA-rey oon POS-to a se-DE-re)

Can I change my reservation?
Posso cambiare la mia prenotazione?
(PO-so kam-BYA-rey la MIA pre-no-ta-TSYO-ne)

BUYING AIRLINE TICKETS

Insert the destination, if applicable

Hi, I'd like to buy a ticket please.
Ciao, vorrei comprare un biglietto per favore.
(chow, vor-REI com-PRAR-re oon big-LIET-to per fa-VO-re)

Can you help me purchase a flight ticket?
Puoi aiutarmi ad acquistare un biglietto aereo?
(pwoi a-yu-TAR-mi ad ak-kwis-TA-re oon big-LIET-to a-E-re-o)

I need to book a flight to [destination].
Ho bisogno di prenotare un volo per [destinazione].
(o bi-SOG-no di pre-no-TA-re oon VO-lo per [ ])

What's the price of a ticket to [destination]?
Qual è il prezzo di un biglietto per [destinazione]?
(kwal e il PREZ-zo di oon big-LIET-to per [ ])

What's the next available flight to [destination]?
Qual è il prossimo volo disponibile per [destinazione]?
(kwal e il PROS-si-mo VO-lo di-spo-NI-bi-le per [ ])

How much is a one-way ticket to [destination]?
Quanto costa un biglietto solo andata per [destinazione]?
(Kwan-to KOS-ta oon big-LIET-to SO-lo an-DA-ta per [ ])

How much is a round-trip ticket to [destination]?
Quanto costa un biglietto andata e ritorno per [destinazione]?
(Kwan-to KOS-ta oon big-LIET-to an-DA-ta e ri-TOR-no per [ ])

Do you have any discounts available?
Avete dei sconti disponibili?
(a-VE-te dei SCON-ti di-spo-NI-bi-li)

Are there any promotions for flights to [destination]?
Ci sono delle promozioni per i voli per [destinazione]?
(chi SO-no DEL-le pro-mo-ZIO-ni per i VO-li per [ ])

Can you tell me about the different fare classes?
Puoi parlarmi delle diverse classi di tariffa?
(pwoi par-LAR-mi DEL-le di-VER-se KLAS-si di tar-IF-fa)

What's the difference between economy and business class?
Qual è la differenza tra classe economica e classe business?
(kwal e la dif-FE-ren-za tra KLAS-se e-ko-NO-mi-ka e KLAS-se BIZ-ness)

Are there any direct flights to [destination]?
Ci sono voli diretti per [destinazione]?
(chi SO-no VO-li di-RET-ti per [ ])

What's the duration of the flight to [destination]?
Quanto dura il volo per [destinazione]?
(Kwan-to DU-ra il VO-lo per [ ])

What's the departure time for the flight to [destination]?
Qual è l'orario di partenza del volo per [destinazione]?
(kwal e lo-RA-rio di PAR-ten-za del VO-lo per [ ])

When's the next flight to [destination]?
Quando è il prossimo volo per [destinazione]?
(Kwan-do e il PROS-si-mo VO-lo per [des-ti-na-ZIO-ne]?)

What's the check-in time for the flight?
Qual è l'orario di check-in per il volo?
(kwal e lo-RA-rio di CHEK-in per il VO-lo)

Can I choose my seat?
Posso scegliere il mio posto?
(POSS-o ske-LYER-re il MIO PO-sto?)

Is there a fee for selecting a seat?
C'è un costo per selezionare un posto?
(che un KOS-to per se-le-tio-NA-re un PO-sto?)

Can I change my flight?
Posso cambiare il mio volo?
(POSS-o kam-BIAR-re il MIO VO-lo?)

Is it possible to get a refund on my ticket?
È possibile ottenere un rimborso sul mio biglietto?
(e pos-SI-bi-le o-TE-ner-re un rim-BOR-so sul MIO big-LIET-to?)

Can I purchase travel insurance?
Posso acquistare un'assicurazione di viaggio?
(POSS-o ak-kwis-TA-re un-as-si-ku-RA-zio-ne di VYAG-gio?)

Is there a limit on the amount of luggage I can bring?
C'è un limite sulla quantità di bagagli che posso portare?
(che un LI-mi-te sul-LA kwan-TI-ta di ba-GA-li ke POSS-o por-TA-re?)

What's the weight limit for luggage?
Qual è il limite di peso per i bagagli?
(kwal e il LI-mi-te di PE-so per i ba-GA-li?)

Is there an extra fee for checked baggage?
C'è un costo extra per i bagagli registrati?
(che un KOS-to EX-tra per i ba-GA-li re-ji-STRAti?)

Can I bring a carry-on bag?
Posso portare un bagaglio a mano?
(POSS-o por-TA-re un ba-GA-lyo a MA-no?)

What's the size limit for carry-on bags?
Qual è il limite di dimensioni per i bagagli a mano?
(kwal e il LI-mi-te di di-MEN-syo-ni per i ba-GA-li a MA-no?)

Can I bring a personal item in addition to my carry-on bag?
Posso portare un oggetto personale oltre al mio bagaglio a mano?
(POSS-o por-TA-re un o-BJET-to per-so-NA-le OL-tre al MIO ba-GA-lyo a MA-no?)

Is there a limit on liquids in my carry-on bag?
C'è un limite sui liquidi nel mio bagaglio a mano?
(che un LI-mi-te sui LI-kwi-di nel MIO ba-GA-lyo a MA-no?)

Where can I find my boarding gate?
Dove posso trovare il mio gate d'imbarco?
(DO-ve POSS-o tro-VAR-re il MIO GA-te diM-BAR-co?)

What's the boarding time for my flight?
Qual è l'orario d'imbarco per il mio volo?
(kwal e lo-RA-rio diM-BAR-ko per il MIO VO-lo?)

Can I get a printed boarding pass?
Pos so avere una carta d'imbarco stampata?
(POSS-o av-VE-re una CAR-ta diM-BAR-ko STAM-pa-ta?)

Can I use an electronic boarding pass?
Posso usare una carta d'imbarco elettronica?
(POSS-o u-SA-re una CAR-ta diM-BAR-ko e-let-TRO-ni-ka?)

Is there a lounge available for passengers?
C'è una sala vip disponibile per i passeggeri?
(che una SA-la VIP dis-po-NI-bi-le per i PAS-se-gheri?)

Can I purchase access to the lounge?
Posso acquistare l'accesso alla sala vip?
(POSS-o ak-kwis-TA-re lac-CEs-so al-LA SA-la VIP?)

Is there Wi-Fi available at the airport?
C'è il Wi-Fi disponibile nell'aeroporto?
(che il WI-Fi dis-po-NI-bi-le nell'AI-ro-por-to?)

Can I charge my electronic devices at the airport?
Posso caricare i miei dispositivi elettronici all'aeroporto?
(POSS-o ka-RI-ka-re i MIEI di-SPO-si-ti-VI e-let-TRO-ni-ci all'AIR-o-por-to?)

Is there a currency exchange at the airport?
C'è un cambio valuta nell'aeroporto?
(che un CAM-bio va-LU-ta nell'ai-ro-por-to?)

Can I use my credit card to pay for things at the airport?
Posso usare la mia carta di credito per pagare le cose all'aeroporto?
*(POSS-o u-SA-re la MIA CAR-ta di CRE-di-to per pa-GA-re le KO-se
all'AI-ro-por-to?)*

Is there a shuttle service to the city center?
C'è un servizio navetta per il centro città?
(che un ser-VE-zio na-VET-ta per il CEN-tro CIT-ta?)

How do I get to the airport/train station/bus station from here?
Come posso arrivare all'aeroporto/stazione ferroviaria/stazione degli
autobus da qui?
*(KO-me POSS-o ar-ri-VA-re all'AIR-o-por-to/sta-ZIO-ne
fe-rro-via-ria/sta-ZIO-ne degli AU-to-bus da kwi?)*

BEING IN AN EMERGENCY SITUATION

Help!
Aiuto!
(ah-YOU-toh!)

Emergency!
Emergenza!
(eh-mehr-JEN-zah!)

I need assistance!
Ho bisogno di assistenza!
(oh bee-ZOHN-yoh dee ahss-ee-STEN-tzah!)

Call for help!
Chiamate il soccorso!
(kyah-MAH-teh eel sok-KOR-soh!)

Please call an ambulance!
Per favore chiamate un'ambulanza!
(pehr fah-VOH-reh kyah-MAH-teh oon ahm-boo-LAHN-tzah!)

I'm in trouble!
Sono in guai!
(SOH-noh een gwai!)

I'm in danger!
Sono in pericolo!
(SOH-noh een peh-REE-koh-loh!)

Somebody help me!
Qualcuno mi aiuti!
(kwahl-KOO-noh mee ah-YOU-tee!)

Please call the police!
Per favore chiamate la polizia!
(pehr fah-VOH-reh kyah-MAH-teh lah poh-LEE-tzee-ah!)

I'm lost!
Sono perso!
(SOH-noh PEHR-soh!)

I'm hurt!
Sono ferito!
(SOH-noh feh-REE-toh!)

I'm injured!
Sono lesionato!
(SOH-noh leh-zee-oh-NAH-toh!)

My passport has been stolen!
Mi hanno rubato il passaporto!
(mee HAHN-noh roo-BAH-toh eel pahs-sah-POR-toh!)

My wallet has been stolen!
Mi hanno rubato il portafoglio!
(mee HAHN-noh roo-BAH-toh eel pohr-tah-FOH-lyoh!)

My bag has been stolen!
Mi hanno rubato la borsa!
(mee HAHN-noh roo-BAH-toh lah BOR-sah!)

My phone has been stolen!
Mi hanno rubato il telefono!
(mee HAHN-noh roo-BAH-toh eel teh-leh-FOH-noh!)

I need medical attention!
Ho bisogno di attenzione medica!
(oh bee-ZOHN-yoh dee aht-ten-ZYOH-neh MEH-dee-kah!)

I need a doctor!
Ho bisogno di un medico!
(oh bee-ZOHN-yoh dee oon MEH-dee-koh!)

I'm having a heart attack!
Sto avendo un infarto!
(sto ah-VEN-doh oon een-FAR-toh!)

I'm having a stroke!
Sto avendo una embolia!
(sto ah-VEN-doh oon-ah em-BOH-lyah!)

I'm feeling sick!
Mi sento male!
(mee SEHN-toh MAH-leh!)

Can you please help me find a hospital?
Potresti aiutarmi a trovare un ospedale?
*(poh-TRES--tee ah-yoo-TAR-mee ah troh-VAH-reh oon
oh-speh-DAH-leh?)*

I'm having an allergic reaction!
Sto avendo una realsione allergica!
(sto ah-VEN-doh oon-ah reh-ah-TSYOH-neh ahl-lehr-JEE-kah!)

I've been bitten by a snake/spider!
Sono stato morso da un serpente/ragno!
(SOH-noh STAH-toh MOR-soh dah oon sehr-PEHN-teh/RAH-nyoh!)

I've been in an accident!
Ho avuto un incidente!
(oh ah-VOO-toh oon een-chi-DEN-teh!)

My car has broken down!
La mia macchina e guasta!
(lah MEE-ah mah-KEE-nah eh GWAH-stah!)

I've missed my flight/train/bus!
Ho perso il mio volo/treno/autobus!
(oh PEHR-soh eel MEE-oh VOH-loh/TREH-noh/OW-toh-boos!)

My accommodation is not safe!
Il mio alloggio non e sicuro!
(eel MEE-oh ahl-LOD-joh nohn eh see-KOO-roh!)

My accommodation has been cancelled!
Il mio alloggio e stato cancellato!
(eel MEE-oh ahl-LOD-joh eh STAH-toh kahn-chel-LAH-toh!)

I need to find a safe place to stay!
Devo trovare un posto sicuro dove stare!
(DEH-vo troh-VAH-reh oon PO-stoh see-KOO-roh DOH-veh STAH-reh!)

My luggage has been lost!
Ho perso I miei bagagli!
(oh PEHR-soh ee MEE-ay bah-GAH-lee!)

My luggage has been damaged!
I miei bagagli sono stati danneggiati!
(ee MEE-ay bah-GAH-lee SOH-noh STAH-tee dahn-neh-DJAH-tee!)

My flight has been cancelled/delayed!
Il mio volo e stato cancellato/ritardato!
(eel MEE-oh VOH-loh eh STAH-toh
kahn-chel-LAH-toh/ree-tahr-DAH-toh!)

I've been robbed!
Sono stato derubato!
(SOH-noh STAH-toh deh-roo-BAH-toh!)

I need to contact my embassy/consulate!
Devo contattare la mia ambasciata/consolato!
(DEH-vo kohn-tah-TAH-reh lah MEE-ah
ahm-bah-SYA-tah/kohn-SOH-lah-toh!)

I need help translating!
Ho bisogno di aiuto per tradurre!
(oh bee-ZOHN-yoh dee ah-YOU-toh pehr trah-DOOR-reh!)

I need to speak to a lawyer!
Devo parlare con un avvocato!
(DEH-vo pahr-LAH-re-kohn oon ahv-vo-KAH-toh!)

I've lost my passport!
Ho perso il mio passaporto!
(oh PEHR-soh eel MEE-oh pah-sah-POR-toh!)

I need to file a police report!
Devo fare una denuncia alla polizia!
(DEH-vo FAH-reh OO-nah deh-NOON-tsyah AHL-lah poh-LEE-tsyah!)

I'm lost and I don't know where I am!
Mi sono perso e non so dove mi trovo!
(mee SOH-noh PEHR-soh eh nohn soh DOH-veh mee TROH-vo!)

ASKING FOR TECH SUPPORT

Can you help me with a technical issue?
Puoi aiutarmi con un problema tecnico?
(PWOI eye-oo-TAHR-mee kohn oon PRO-ble-mah TEK-nee-koh?)

I'm having trouble with my computer.
Ho dei problemi con il mio computer.
(oh deh-EE pro-BLE-mee kohn eel MEE-oh kohm-POO-ter)

My device isn't working properly.
Il mio dispositivo non funziona correttamente.
*(eel MEE-oh dee-vee-SEE-po non foon-tsee-OH-nah
kohr-rett-tah-MEN-teh)*

I can't access the internet.
Non riesco ad accedere a Internet.
(non ree-YES-koh ahd aht-CHEH-deh-reh ah een-ter-NET)

I'm getting an error message.
Sto ricevendo un messaggio di errore.
(sto ree-cheh-VEN-doh oon meh-SAH-joh dee EH-ror-reh)

My computer is running slow.
Il mio computer è lento.
(eel MEE-oh kohm-POO-ter eh LEHN-toh)

I can't connect to my printer.
Non riesco a collegarmi alla stampante.
(non ree-YES-koh ah ko-lleh-GAR-mee AH-lah stam-PEHN-teh)

I need help installing software.
Ho bisogno di aiuto per installare un software.
*(oh bee-SOH-nyoh dee eye-YOO-toh pehr een-stah-LAH-reh oon
soff-twair)*

My screen is frozen.
La mia schermata è bloccata.
(lah MEE-ah skher-MAH-tah eh BLOK-kah-tah)

My device won't turn on.
Il mio dispositivo non si accende.
(eel MEE-oh dee-vee-SEE-po non see ah-CHEHN-deh)

I'm having trouble with my email.
Ho problemi con la mia email.
(oh pro-BLE-mee kohn lah MEE-ah ee-mayl)

My keyboard isn't working.
La mia tastiera non funziona.
(lah MEE-ah tah-STYEH-rah non foon-tsee-OH-nah)

My mouse isn't responding.
Il mio mouse non risponde.
(eel MEE-oh moo-SEH non ree-SPON-deh)

I need help with a password reset.
Ho bisogno di aiuto per reimpostare la password.
(oh bee-SOH-nyoh dee eye-YOO-toh pehr ray-IM-poh-stah-reh lah PAHS-sword)

I can't open a file.
Non riesco ad aprire un file.
(non ree-YES-koh ahd ah-PREE-reh oon FEE-leh)

My device is overheating.
Il mio dispositivo si surriscalda.
(eel MEE-oh dee-vee-SEE-po see soo-ree-skahl-dah)

My webcam isn't working.
La mia webcam non funziona.
(lah MEE-ah web-KAM non foon-tsee-OH-nah)

I'm having trouble with my microphone.
Ho problemi con il mio microfono.
(oh pro-BLE-mee kohn eel MEE-oh MEE-kro-foh-no)

My speakers aren't working.
Le mie casse non funzionano.
(leh MEE-eh KAHS-seh non foon-tsee-OH-nah-no)

My device keeps crashing.
Il mio dispositivo si blocca continuamente.
(eel MEE-oh dee-vee-SEE-po see BLOK-kah kohn-too-ee-NAH-men-teh)

My internet is slow.
La mia connessione Internet è lenta.
(lah MEE-ah kohn-neh-SYOH-neh een-ter-NET eh LEHN-tah)

I can't access my files.
Non riesco ad accedere ai miei file.
(non ree-YES-koh ahd aht-CHEH-deh-reh eye MEE-eh FEE-leh)

My device is infected with a virus.
Il mio dispositivo è infetto da un virus.
(eel MEE-oh dee-vee-SEE-po eh een-FEH-toh dah oon VEE-roos)

I need help with a software update.
Ho bisogno di aiuto per l'aggiornamento del software.
(oh bee-SOH-nyoh dee eye-YOO-toh pehr ladj-YOR-nah-men-toh del soff-twair)

My device is making strange noises.
Il mio dispositivo emette rumori strani.
(eel MEE-oh dee-vee-SEE-po eh-MEH-teh roo-MOH-ree STRAH-nee)

I'm having trouble with my wireless network.
Ho problemi con la mia rete wireless.
(oh pro-BLE-mee kohn lah MEE-ah REH-teh WAI-reh-lehs)

My device is displaying an error code.
Il mio dispositivo sta visualizzando un codice di errore.
(eel MEE-oh dee-vee-SEE-po stah vee-zoo-ah-LEE-zahn-doh oon koh-DEE-tcheh dee EH-ror-reh)

I need help with data backup.
Ho bisogno di aiuto per il backup dei dati.
(oh bee-SOH-nyoh dee eye-YOO-toh pehr eel BAHK-kup dei DAH-tee)

My device isn't recognizing a peripheral.
Il mio dispositivo non riconosce un periferico.
*(eel MEE-oh dee-vee-SEE-po non ree-ko-NOSH-cheh oon
peh-ree-FEH-ree-koh)*

My device won't charge.
Il mio dispositivo non si carica.
(eel MEE-oh dee-vee-SEE-po non see kah-RAH-kah)

I need help with a software installation.
Ho bisogno di aiuto per l'installazione del software.
*(oh bee-SOH-nyoh dee eye-YOO-toh pehr lins-tah-LAH-tsyoh-neh del
soff-twair)*

My device won't boot up.
Il mio dispositivo non si avvia.
(eel MEE-oh dee-vee-SEE-po non see AHV-vee-ah)

My device is running out of storage space.
Il mio dispositivo sta esaurendo lo spazio di archiviazione.
*(eel MEE-oh dee-vee-po stah eh-sow-REHN-doh loh SPAH-tsee-oh dee
ar-kee-VEE-ah-TSYOH-neh)*

I need help with setting up a new device.
Ho bisogno di aiuto per configurare un nuovo dispositivo.
*(oh bee-SOH-nyoh dee eye-YOO-toh pehr kohn-fee-goo-RAH-reh oon
NOO-vo dee-vee-SEE-po)*

My device is overheating.
Il mio dispositivo si surriscalda.
(eel MEE-oh dee-vee-SEE-po see soo-ree-skahl-dah)

I can't connect to a particular website.
Non riesco a connettermi a un particolare sito web.
*(non ree-YES-koh ah kohn-neh-TEHR-mee ah oon par-tee-KOH-lah-reh
SEE-toh web)*

My device is frozen.

Il mio dispositivo si è bloccato.

(eel MEE-oh dee-vee-SEE-po see eh BLOK-kah-toh)

I need help with password recovery.

Ho bisogno di aiuto per il recupero della password.

(oh bee-SOH-nyoh dee eye-YOO-toh pehr eel reh-KOO-peh-roh della pahs-WORD)

My device won't turn on.

Il mio dispositivo non si accende.

(eel MEE-oh dee-vee-SEE-po non see ah-CHEHN-deh)

I need help with troubleshooting a problem.

Ho bisogno di aiuto per risolvere un problema.

(oh bee-SOH-nyoh dee eye-YOO-toh pehr ree-SOL-veh-reh oon pro-BLE-mah)

CASUAL CONVERSATION AND SMALL TALK

Hey, how's it going?
Ciao, come va?
(chow, KOM-eh-vah?)

What have you been up to lately?
Cosa hai fatto ultimamente?
(KOH-zah hai FAT-toh ul-tee-mah-MEN-teh?)

Nice to see you again.
Piacere di rivederti.
(pyah-CHE-reh dee ree-VEH-der-tee)

How was your day?
Come è andata la tua giornata?
(KOH-meh eh ahn-DAH-tah lah TOO-ah jor-NAH-tah?)

What's new with you?
Cosa c'è di nuovo con te?
(KOH-zah cheh dee NOO-vo kon teh?)

How's your family doing?
Come sta la tua famiglia?
(KOH-meh stah lah TOO-ah fah-MEE-lyah?)

Did you catch the game last night?
Hai visto la partita ieri sera?
(hai VEE-stoh lah par-TEE-tah YEH-ree seh-rah?)

What are your plans for the weekend?
Quali sono i tuoi programmi per il weekend?
(KWAH-lee SOH-noh ee TOO-ee proh-GRAM-mee pehr eel WEE-kend?)

Have you seen any good movies or TV shows recently?
Hai visto qualche bel film o programma TV di recente?
(hai VEE-stoh KWAHL-kweh bel FEELM oh proh-GRAHM-mah TV dee reh-CHEN-teh?)

How's work been treating you?
Come va il lavoro?
(KOH-meh vah eel lah-VOH-roh?)

What do you like to do in your free time?
Cosa ti piace fare nel tempo libero?
(KOH-zah tee PYAH-cheh FAH-reh nel TEM-poh LEH-beh-roh?)

How's the weather treating you today?
Come va il tempo oggi?
(KOH-meh vah eel TEM-poh O-jee?)

What's your favorite type of food?
Qual è il tuo tipo di cibo preferito?
(KWAH-leh eel TOO-oh TEE-po dee CHEE-boh preh-feh-REE-toh?)

Have you been on any vacations recently?
Hai fatto delle vacanze di recente?
(hai FAT-toh DEL-leh vah-KAN-zeh dee reh-CHEN-teh?)

Do you have any pets?
Hai degli animali domestici?
(hai DEH-zjoh ah-nee-MAH-lee doh-MEH-stee-chee?)

What's your favorite book or author?
Qual è il tuo libro o autore preferito?
(KWAH-leh eel TOO-oh LEE-broh oh au-TOH-reh preh-feh-REE-toh?)

Have you tried any new restaurants lately?
Hai provato qualche nuovo ristorante di recente?
(hai proh-VAH-toh KWAHL-kweh NOO-vo rees-toh-RAHN-teh dee reh-CHEN-teh?)

What kind of music do you like to listen to?
Che tipo di musica ti piace ascoltare?
(keh TEE-po dee MOO-zee-kah tee PYAH-cheh ah-skohl-TAH-reh?)

How do you typically spend your evenings?
Come di solito trascorri le tue serate?
(KOH-meh dee soh-LEE-toh trah-SCORE-ree leh TOO-eh seh-RAH-teh?)

What's your favorite hobby or pastime?
Qual è il tuo hobby o passatempo preferito?
(KWAH-leh eh eel TOO-oh OH-bee oh pahs-sah-TEHM-poh preh-feh-REE-toh?)

Have you visited any interesting places lately?
Hai visitato posti interessanti di recente?
(hai vee-ZEE-tah-toh POH-stee een-teh-reh-SAHN-tee dee reh-CHEN-teh?)

How do you like your job?
Ti piace il tuo lavoro?
(tee PYAH-cheh eel TOO-oh lah-VOH-roh?)

What's your favorite type of art?
Qual è il tuo tipo di arte preferito?
(KWAH-leh eh eel TOO-oh TEE-po dee AR-teh preh-feh-REE-toh?)

Have you read any good books recently?
Hai letto qualche bel libro di recente?
(hai LET-toh KWAHL-kweh bel LEE-broh dee reh-CHEN-teh?)

What kind of sports do you enjoy watching or playing?
Che tipo di sport ti piace guardare o praticare?
(keh TEE-po dee sport tee PYAH-cheh GWAHR-dah-reh oh pra-TEE-kah-reh?)

How's your day been so far?
Come è andata la tua giornata finora?
(KOH-meh eh ahn-DAH-tah lah TOO-ah jor-NAH-tah fee-NOH-rah?)

What's your favorite TV show?
Qual è il tuo programma TV preferito?
(KWAH-leh eh eel TOO-oh proh-GRAHM-mah TV preh-feh-REE-toh?)

Have you been to any concerts lately?
Sei stato a qualche concerto di recente?
(sey STAH-toh ah KWAHL-kweh kohn-CHER-toh dee reh-CHEN-teh?)

How do you like to celebrate your birthday?
Come ti piace festeggiare il tuo compleanno?
(KOH-meh tee PYAH-cheh feh-stehd-JAH-reh eel TOO-oh kohm-pleh-AN-noh?)

What's your favorite type of drink?
Qual è il tuo tipo di bevanda preferito?
(KWAH-leh eh eel TOO-oh TEE-po dee beh-VAHN-dah preh-feh-REE-toh?)

Have you been to any interesting events recently?
Sei stato a qualche evento interessante di recente?
(sey STAH-toh ah KWAHL-kweh eh-VEHN-toh een-teh-reh-SAHN-teh dee reh-CHEN-teh?)

Do you have any travel plans coming up?
Hai programmi di viaggio in arrivo?
(hai proh-GRAHM-mee dee vee-AH-joh een ah-REE-voh?)

What's your favorite type of food?
Qual è il tuo tipo di cibo preferito?
(KWAH-leh eh eel TOO-oh TEE-po dee CHEE-boh preh-feh-REE-toh?)

Have you seen any good movies lately?
Hai visto qualche bel film di recente?
(hai VEE-zoh KWAHL-kweh bel FEELM dee reh-CHEN-teh?)

How do you like to stay active or exercise?
Come ti piace rimanere attivo o fare esercizio?
(KOH-meh tee PYAH-cheh ree-mah-NEH-reh AHK-tee-voh oh FAH-reh eh-ser-CHEE-tzee-oh?)

What's your favorite type of weather?
Qual è il tuo tipo di clima preferito?
(KWAH-leh eh eel TOO-oh TEE-po dee KLEE-mah preh-feh-REE-toh?)

Have you been to any new restaurants recently?
Sei stato in qualche nuovo ristorante di recente?
(sey STAH-toh een KWAHL-kweh NWOH-vo ree-stoh-RAHN-teh dee reh-CHEN-teh?)

How do you like to relax or unwind?
Come ti piace rilassarti o riposarti?
(KOH-meh tee PYAH-cheh ree-lah-SAHR-tee oh ree-poh-SAHR-tee?)

How do you like to stay active?
Come ti piace rimanere attivo?
(KOH-meh tee PYAH-cheh ree-mah-NEH-reh AHK-tee-voh?)

How do you like to spend your weekends?
Come ti piace trascorrere i tuoi weekend?
(KOH-meh tee PYAH-cheh trah-skoh-REH-reh ee TOO-oh-ee WEE-kend?)

BEING ON A DATE

Are you single?
Sei single?
(SEH-ee SEEHN-gleh?)

Would you like to grab a drink?
Ti va di prendere qualcosa da bere?
(tee vah dee pren-DEH-reh kwa-LKO-sa dah BEH-reh?)

What are your interests?
Quali sono i tuoi interessi?
(KWAH-lee SOH-noh ee TOH-ee in-teh-RES-see?)

Can I get your number?
Posso avere il tuo numero?
(POH-soh ah-VEH-reh eel TOO-oh NOO-meh-roh?)

Do you want to go out sometime?
Vuoi uscire qualche volta?
(VWOH-ee oo-SHEE-reh KWAHL-ke-vohl-ta?)

Let's grab dinner sometime.
Prendiamo una cena insieme un giorno.
(prehn-DEE-ah-moh OO-nah CHEH-nah een-SEE-meh oon GOR-noh?)

I've had a great time with you.
Mi sono divertito molto con te.
(mee SOH-noh dee-vehr-TEE-toh MOHL-toh kon teh?)

Can I see you again?
Posso rivederti?
(POH-soh ree-VEH-dehr-tee?)

What do you like to do for fun?
Cosa ti piace fare per divertirti?
(KOH-sah tee pee-AH-cheh FAH-reh pehr dee-VEHR-teer-tee?)

Would you like to go for a walk?
Ti va di fare una passeggiata?
(tee vah dee FAH-reh OO-nah pahs-seh-DJAH-tah?)

Do you have any plans this weekend?
Hai dei programmi per questo fine settimana?
*(AH-ee deh-ee proh-GRAHM-mee pehr KWES-toh FEE-neh
SET-tee-MAH-nah?)*

I think you're really cute.
Penso che sei davvero carino/a.
(PEHN-soh keh SEH-ee DAH-ver-roh kah-REE-noh/ah?)

Let's go out and have some fun.
Usciamo e divertiamoci.
(oo-SHYAH-moh eh dee-vehr-tee-AH-moh-chee?)

What kind of music do you like?
Che tipo di musica ti piace?
(keh TEE-poh dee moo-ZEE-kah tee pee-AH-cheh?)

Let's go to a movie together.
Andiamo al cinema insieme.
(ahn-DEE-ah-moh ahl chee-NEH-mah een-SEE-meh?)

Have you ever been to this restaurant?
Sei mai stato/a in questo ristorante?
(SEH-ee mah-ee STAH-toh/ah een KWEH-stoh ree-stoh-RAHN-teh?)

I would love to get to know you better.
Mi piacerebbe conoscerti meglio.
(mee pee-ah-cheh-REHB-beh koh-noh-SHEHR-tee MEH-lyoh?)

Do you want to dance?
Vuoi ballare?
(VWOH-ee bahl-LAH-reh?)

What's your favorite food?
Qual è il tuocibo preferito?
(KWAH-lee eel TOO-oh CHEE-boh preh-feh-REE-toh?)

Let's go for a drive.
Andiamo a fare un giro in macchina.
(ahn-DEE-ah-moh ah FAH-reh oon JEE-roh een mahk-KEE-nah?)

Can I buy you a drink?
Posso offrirti da bere?
(POH-soh ohf-FREER-tee dah BEH-reh?)

Would you like to go to a concert?
Ti va di andare a un concerto?
(tee vah dee ahn-DAH-reh ah oon kohn-CHEHR-toh?)

You have a great sense of humor.
Hai un grande senso dell'umorismo.
(AH-ee oon GRAHN-deh SEN-soh dehl-loo-moh-REES-moh?)

Let's go to the beach together.
Andiamo in spiaggia insieme.
(ahn-DEE-ah-moh een SPYAH-jah een-SEE-meh?)

What's your favorite book?
Qual è il tuo libro preferito?
(KWAH-lee eel TOO-oh LEE-broh preh-feh-REE-toh?)

Can I hold your hand?
Posso tenerti per mano?
(POH-soh teh-NEHR-tee pehr MAH-noh?)

Let's go for a bike ride.
Andiamo a fare un giro in bici.
(ahn-DEE-ah-moh ah FAH-reh oon JEE-roh een BEE-chee?)

I really enjoyed our conversation.
Ho apprezzato molto la nostra conversazione.
*(oh ap-preh-TSAH-toh MOHL-toh lah NOH-strah
kohn-ver-saht-zyoh-NEH?)*

Can I kiss you?
Posso baciarti?
(POH-soh bah-CYAHR-tee?)

What's your favorite hobby?
Qual è il tuo hobby preferito?
(KWAH-lee eel TOO-oh OH-bee preh-feh-REE-toh?)

Let's go to a museum.
Andiamo in un museo.
(ahn-DEE-ah-moh een oon moo-ZEH-oh?)

You have a beautiful smile.
Hai un sorriso bellissimo.
(AH-ee oon sohr-REE-zoh behl-LEES-see-moh?)

Can I take you out on a picnic?
Posso portarti a fare un picnic?
(POH-soh pohr-TAHR-tee ah FAH-reh oon pee-KNEEK?)

I love spending time with you.
Mi piace passare del tempo con te.
(mee pee-AH-cheh pahs-SAH-reh dehl TEHM-poh kon teh?)

Let's go for a hike.
Andiamo a fare un'escursione.
(ahn-DEE-ah-moh ah FAH-reh oon EH-skoor-see-OH-neh?)

What's your favorite movie?
Qual è il tuo film preferito?
(KWAH-lee eel TOO-oh feelm preh-feh-REE-toh?)

I think you're beautiful/handsome.
Penso che tu sia bellissima/bellissimo.
(PEHN-soh keh too SEE-ah behl-LEE-see-mah/ behl-LEE-see-moh)

41

Let's go dancing.
Andiamo a ballare.
(ahn-DEE-ah-moh ah bahl-LAH-reh)

You make me happy.
Mi fai felice.
(mee fai FEH-lee-cheh)

Can I show you around town?
Posso farti vedere la città?
(POH-soh FAHR-tee veh-DEH-reh lah CHEET-tah?)

SHOPPING AT A CLOTHING STORE

Do you offer alterations or tailoring services?
Offrite servizi di sartoria o di sartoria su misura?
(ohf-FREE-teh sehr-VEE-tsee dee sar-TOH-ree-ah oh dee
sar-TOH-ree-ah soo mee-SOO-rah)

How long is your return policy?
Quanto tempo ho per restituire il prodotto?
(KWAN-toh TEHM-poh oh pehr reh-stee-TEER-eh eel proh-DOHT-toh)

Can I see that in a different color?
Posso vedere questo in un colore diverso?
(PAH-soh veh-DEH-reh KWEH-stoh een oon KOH-loh-reh dee-VEHR-soh)

Do you have any sales going on right now?
Ci sono sconti in corso al momento?
(CHEE SOH-noh SKON-tee een KOR-soh ahl moh-MEN-toh)

How many items can I take to the fitting room?
Quanti capi posso portare in camerino?
(KWAN-tee KA-pee PAH-soh por-TAH-reh een kah-meh-REE-noh)

Can I pay with cash or credit card?
Posso pagare in contanti o con la carta di credito?
(PAH-soh pah-GAH-reh een kohn-TAHN-tee oh kon lah KAR-tah dee
kre-DEE-toh)

Can I get a gift receipt?
Posso avere una ricevuta regalo?
(PAH-soh ah-VEH-reh OO-nah ree-cheh-VOO-tah reh-GAH-loh)

Are there any additional fees?
Ci sono costi aggiuntivi?
(CHEE SOH-noh KOH-stee adj-OON-tee-vee)

Is there a sale section?
C'è una sezione saldi?
(CHEH OO-nah seh-TSYOH-neh SAHL-dee)

Can I try on multiple items at once?
Posso provare più capi contemporaneamente?
(PAH-soh proh-VAH-reh pyoo KA-pee kon-tehm-poh-ra-neh-MEN-teh)

Can I return an item if it doesn't fit?
Posso restituire un capo se non mi va bene?
(PAH-soh reh-stee-TWEE-reh oon KA-po seh non mee vah BEH-neh)

Do you have this in a smaller/larger size?
Ce l'ha in una taglia più piccola/grande?
(Cheh lhah een OO-nah TA-lyah pyoo pee-KOH-lah/GRAN-deh)

Can you help me find a certain style?
Può aiutarmi a trovare uno stile particolare?
*(Pwoh ah-yoo-TAHR-mee ah troh-VAH-reh OO-noh stee-leh
par-tee-koh-LAH-reh)*

Can I reserve an item and come back for it later?
Posso prenotare un capo e ritirarlo dopo?
(PAH-soh preh-noh-TAH-reh oon KA-po eh ree-tee-RAHR-loh DOH-poh)

Can you recommend something to wear for a special occasion?
Può consigliarmi qualcosa da indossare per un'occasione speciale?
*(Pwoh kohn-see-LYAR-mee kwahl-KOH-sah dah een-DOHSS-ah-reh
pehr oon-oh-KKA-zee-OH-neh speh-CHEE-leh)*

Do you have a fitting room available?
C'è un camerino disponibile?
(Cheh oon kah-meh-REE-noh dee-SPOH-nee-bee-leh)

Can I return an item if I change my mind?
Posso restituire un capo se cambio idea?
(PAH-soh reh-stee-TWEE-reh oon KA-po seh KAHM-bee-oh EE-deh-ah)

Sure, I'm looking for this shirt in size medium. Do you have it?

Certamente, cerco questa camicia taglia media. Ce l'ha?

(Chehr-tah-MEHN-teh, CHEHR-koh KWEH-stah kah-MEE-chah TAH-lyah MEH-dee-ah. Cheh lhah?)

PAYING FOR ITEMS

How much is it?
Quanto costa?
(KWAN-toh KO-sta)

How much do I owe you?
Quanto le devo?
(KWAN-toh leh DEH-vo)

What's the total?
Quanto fa in tutto?
(KWAN-toh fa in TUT-to)

Can you tell me the price?
Puoi dirmi il prezzo?
(PWOY DEER-mee eel PRET-zoh)

How much does this cost?
Quanto costa questo?
(KWAN-toh KO-sta KWES-toh)

What's the damage?
Quanto è il danno?
(KWAN-toh eh eel DAN-no)

Could you give me the bill, please?
Potresti darmi il conto, per favore?
(po-TRES-tee DAR-mee eel KON-toh, per fa-VO-re)

May I see the receipt?
Posso vedere lo scontrino?
(POS-so vede-REH lo SKON-tree-no)

Could you tell me the final price?
Potresti dirmi il prezzo finale?
(po-TRES-tee DEER-mee eel PRET-zoh fi-NA-leh)

How much should I pay?
Quanto devo pagare?
(KWAN-toh DEH-vo pa-GA-reh)

Is this the right amount?
È questa la cifra giusta?
(eh KWE-sta la TSEE-fra JWO-sta)

Can I pay with cash?
Posso pagare in contanti?
(POS-so pa-GA-reh in kon-TAN-tee)

Do you accept credit cards?
Accettate carte di credito?
(atch-ET-ta-te KAR-teh dee kre-DEE-to)

Can I pay with my debit card?
Posso pagare con la carta di debito?
(POS-so pa-GA-reh kon la KAR-ta dee DE-bee-to)

Can I pay with a check?
Posso pagare con un assegno?
(POS-so pa-GA-reh kon oon AS-se-nyo)

Do you take Apple Pay?
Accettate Apple Pay?
(atch-ET-ta-te APPLE Pay)

Can I pay by PayPal?
Posso pagare con PayPal?
(POS-so pa-GA-reh kon PayPal)

Can I use a gift card to pay for this?
Posso usare una carta regalo per pagare questo?
(POS-so oo-SA-reh OO-na KAR-ta re-GA-lo per pa-GA-reh KWES-to)

Can I split the bill?
Posso dividere il conto?
(POS-so di-ve-DEH-reh eel KON-to)

Can you charge it to my account?
Puoi addebitarlo sul mio conto?
(PWOY ad-dee-BEE-tar-lo sul MEE-o KON-to)

Can I have a student discount?
Posso avere uno sconto studenti?
(POS-so a-VEH-reh OO-no SCON-toh stoo-DEN-tee)

Can I have a senior discount?
Posso avere uno sconto anziani?
(POS-so a-VEH-reh OO-no SCON-toh an-TSA-nee)

Can I have a military discount?
Posso avere uno sconto militari?
(POS-so a-VEH-reh OO-no SCON-toh mee-lee-TA-ree)

Can I have a coupon?
Posso avere un coupon?
(POS-so a-VEH-reh oon KOO-pon)

Can I redeem my loyalty points?
Posso usare i miei punti fedeltà?
(POS-so oo-SA-reh ee MEE-eh-ee POON-tee feh-del-TA)

How much is the tax?
Quanto è la tassa?
(KWAN-toh eh la TAS-sa)

Is the tax included in the price?
La tassa è inclusa nel prezzo?
(la TAS-sa eh in-CLOO-sa nel PRET-zoh)

What's the service charge?
Quanto è il servizio?
(KWAN-toh eh eel ser-VEE-tsee-yo)

Is there a gratuity included?
C'è incluso il servizio?
(cheh in-CLOO-so eel ser-VEE-tsee-yo)

Can I add a tip?
Posso lasciare una mancia?
(POS-so la-shee-A-reh OO-na MAN-tcha)

How much should I tip?
Quanto dovrei lasciare di mancia?
(KWAN-toh doh-VREI la-shee-A-reh dee MAN-tcha)

Do you have change for a $20 bill?
Avete il resto per un biglietto da 20 dollari?
(a-VEH-teh eel RES-to per oon bil-YET-toh da ven-TO-reh DOL-la-ree)

Can you break a $50 bill?
Potresti farmi il resto per un biglietto da 50 dollari?
(po-TRES-tee FAR-mee eel RES-to per oon bil-YET-toh da chin-KWAN-ta DOL-la-ree)

Can I have a receipt, please?
Posso avere la ricevuta, per favore?
(POS-so a-VEH-reh la ree-che-VU-ta, per fa-VO-re)

Can I get a copy of the receipt?
Posso avere una copia della ricevuta?
(POS-so a-VEH-reh OO-na KO-pya DEL-la ree-che-VU-ta)

Can you email me the receipt?
Puoi mandarmi la ricevuta via email?
(PWOY man-DAR-mee la ree-che-VU-ta VEE-ya ee-MAYL)

Can you put it in a bag, please?
Potresti metterlo in una borsa, per favore?
(po-TRES-tee meh-TAIR-lo in OO-na BOR-sa, per fa-VO-re)

Thank you very much.
Grazie mille.
(GRA-tsee-EH MEE-leh)

Do you accept credit cards?

Accettate le carte di credito?

(at-cheh-TA-teh le CAR-teh dee cre-DEE-toh)

Do you offer any discounts?

Offerite degli sconti?

(off-REE-teh dehl-ee SCON-tee)

SIMPLE ANSWERS TO THE MOST COMMON QUESTIONS

Yes, I agree.
Sì, sono d'accordo.
(SEE, SO-noh dah-KOR-do)

No, I disagree.
No, non sono d'accordo.
(NOH, non SO-noh dah-KOR-do)

I don't know.
Non lo so.
(NON loh SOH)

Maybe.
Forse.
(FOR-seh)

I'm not sure.
Non sono sicuro/sicura.
(NON SO-noh see-KOO-roh/see-KOO-rah)

That's a good question.
È una buona domanda.
(EH OO-nah BWOH-nah doh-MAN-dah)

It depends.
Dipende.
(dee-PEN-deh)

I think so.
Penso di sì.
(PEN-soh dee SEE)

I don't think so.
Penso di no.
(PEN-soh dee NOH)

I'm not really sure what you're asking.
Non sono sicuro/sicura di quello che stai chiedendo.
*(NON SO-noh see-KOO-roh/see-KOO-rah dee KWE-loh keh STAI
kee-EDEN-doh)*

I'm sorry, I didn't catch that. Could you repeat the question?
Mi dispiace, non ho capito. Potresti ripetere la domanda?
*(mee dees-pee-AH-cheh, non oh ka-PEE-toh. poh-TREH-stee
ree-peh-TEH-reh lah doh-MAN-dah)*

I'm sorry, I'm not able to answer that question.
Mi dispiace, non sono in grado di rispondere a quella domanda.
*(mee dees-pee-AH-cheh, non SO-noh een GRAH-deh dee
ree-SPOHN-deh-reh ah KWE-lah doh-MAN-dah)*

Let me get back to you on that.
Fammi pensare e ti rispondo.
(FA-mee pen-SA-reh eh tee ree-SPON-do)

I'm sorry, I'm not qualified to answer that question.
Mi dispiace, non sono qualificato/qualificata per rispondere a quella
domanda.
*(mee dees-pee-AH-cheh, non SO-noh
kwa-lee-fee-KAH-toh/kwa-lee-fee-KAH-tah per ree-SPOHN-deh-reh ah
KWE-lah doh-MAN-dah)*

I'll have to think about it.
Ci devo pensare.
(chee DEH-vo pen-SA-reh)

That's a tough question.
È una domanda difficile.
(EH OO-nah doh-MAN-dah dee-fee-CHI-leh)

I'm not comfortable answering that question.
Non mi sento a mio agio a rispondere a quella domanda.
(non mee SEN-toh ah MEE-oh AH-joh ah ree-SPOHN-deh-reh ah KWE-lah doh-MAN-dah)

I don't have an opinion on that.
Non ho un'opinione in merito.
(non oh oon oh-pee-nyoh-neh een MEH-ree-toh)

I'll have to pass on that.
Devo declinare.
(DEH-vo deh-klee-NAH-reh)

I'm sorry, I'm not the right person to answer that question.
Mi dispiace, non sono la persona giusta per rispondere a quella domanda.
(mee dees-pee-AH-cheh, non SO-noh lah per-SOH-nah JYOO-stah per ree-SPOHN-deh-reh ah KWE-lah doh-MAN-dah)

I don't have enough information to answer that.
Non ho abbastanza informazioni per rispondere a quella domanda.
(non oh ab-ba-STAN-sah een-for-ma-tsee-OH-nee per ree-SPOHN-deh-reh ah KWE-lah doh-MAN-dah)

I'm sorry, I'm not fluent in Italian.
Mi dispiace, non parlo fluentemente l'italiano.
(mee dees-pee-AH-cheh, non PAR-loh floo-en-teh-MEN-teh lee-ta-LYA-noh)

I'll do my best to answer that.
Farò del mio meglio per rispondere a quella domanda.
(fa-ROH del MEE-oh ME-lyoh per ree-SPOHN-deh-reh ah KWE-lah doh-MAN-dah)

Can you please rephrase the question?
Puoi riphrasare la domanda per favore?
(pwoy ree-FRA-sa-reh lah doh-MAN-dah per fa-VO-reh)

I'm sorry, I don't understand the question.
Mi dispiace, non capisco la domanda.
(mee dees-pee-AH-cheh, non ka-PEES-koh lah doh-MAN-dah)

That's an interesting question.
È una domanda interessante.
(EH OO-nah doh-MAN-dah een-ter-ES-san-teh)

I'm sorry, I don't have the answer to that.
Mi dispiace, non ho la risposta a quella domanda.
(mee dees-pee-AH-cheh, non oh lah ree-SPOS-tah ah KWE-lah doh-MAN-dah)

I'm not familiar with that topic.
Non sono familiare con quell'argomento.
(non SO-noh fa-mee-LYA-reh kon KWE-lar-goh-MEN-toh)

I'm sorry, I need more information to answer that.
Mi dispiace, ho bisogno di più informazioni per rispondere a quella domanda.
(mee dees-pee-AH-cheh, oh bee-SO-nyoh dee PEE-oo een-for-ma-tsee-OH-nee per ree-SPOHN-deh-reh ah KWE-lah doh-MAN-dah)

I'm sorry, I'm not comfortable discussing that.
Mi dispiace, non mi sento a mio agio a parlare di questo.
(mee dees-pee-AH-cheh, non mee SEN-toh ah MEE-oh AH-joh ah par-LA-reh dee KWES-toh)

I'm sorry, I don't have the expertise to answer that.
Mi dispiace, non ho le competenze per rispondere a quella domanda.
(mee dees-pee-AH-cheh, non oh leh kohm-pe-TEN-tseh per ree-SPOHN-deh-reh ah KWE-lah doh-MAN-dah)

I'm not sure, but I can find out for you.
Non sono sicuro, ma posso scoprirlo per te.
(non SO-noh see-KOO-roh, mah POH-soh skohp-PEER-loh per teh)

I'm sorry, I don't have the time right now.
Mi dispiace, non ho il tempo adesso.
(mee dees-pee-AH-cheh, non oh eel TEM-po ah-DESS-soh)

I'm not sure, let me double-check.
Non sono sicuro, fammi controllare ancora una volta.
(non SO-noh see-KOO-roh, FA-mee kon-troh-LA-reh an-KOH-ra OO-nah VOL-tah)

I'm sorry, I don't feel comfortable answering that.
Mi dispiace, non mi sento a mio agio a rispondere a quella domanda.
(mee dees-pee-AH-cheh, non mee SEN-toh ah MEE-oh AH-joh ah ree-SPOHN-deh-reh ah KWE-lah doh-MAN-dah)

I'm not qualified to answer that.
Non sono qualificato per rispondere a quella domanda.
(non SO-noh kwa-lee-fee-KAH-toh per ree-SPOHN-deh-reh ah KWE-lah doh-MAN-dah)

I'm sorry, I don't know the answer.
Mi dispiace, non conosco la risposta.
(mee dees-pee-AH-cheh, non koh-NOH-skoh lah ree-SPOS-tah)

I'm not the best person to ask about that.
Non sono la persona migliore a cui chiedere informazioni su questo.
(non SO-noh lah per-SOH-nah mee-LYOH-reh ah KOO-ee kee-DEH-reh een-for-ma-tsee-OH-nee soo KWES-toh)

I'm sorry, I don't have the authority to answer that.
Mi dispiace, non ho l'autorità per rispondere a quella domanda.
(mee dees-pee-AH-cheh, non oh law-toh-REE-tah per ree-SPOHN-deh-reh ah KWE-lah doh-MAN-dah)

I'm not sure, I'll need to look into it.
Non sono sicuro, dovrò approfondire.
(non SO-noh see-KOO-roh, DOH-vroh ap-proh-FEEN-dee-reh)

ASKING FOR AND GIVING DIRECTIONS

Insert the location, if applicable

Excuse me, can you help me find my way?
Mi scusi, può aiutarmi a trovare la strada?
(mee SKOO-see, PWOH AY-yoo-tar-mee ah troh-VAH-reh lah STRA-da?)

Could you tell me where [location] is?
Potrebbe dirmi dove si trova [location]?
(poh-TREB-beh DEER-mee DOH-veh see TROH-vah [ ]?)

I'm lost, can you point me in the right direction?
Mi sono perso/a, può indicarmi la giusta direzione?
(mee SOH-noh PEHR-soh/ah, PWOH een-dee-KAHR-mee lah JYOO-sta dee-reh-TSYOH-neh?)

How do I get to [location] from here?
Come arrivo a [location] da qui?
(KOH-meh ah-REE-voh ah [ ] dah kwee?)

I'm trying to find [location]. Could you help me with directions?
Sto cercando [location]. Potrebbe aiutarmi con le indicazioni?
(sto cher-KAHN-doh [ ]. poh-TREB-beh ay-yoo-TAR-mee kohn leh een-dee-KAH-tsee-oh-nee?)

Which way do I need to go to get to [location]?
In quale direzione devo andare per arrivare a [location]?
(een kWA-leh dee-reh-TSYOH-neh DEH-voh ahn-DAH-reh pehr ah-REE-vah-reh ah [ ]?)

Can you give me directions to [location]?
Potrebbe darmi le indicazioni per [location]?
(poh-TREB-beh DARM-mee leh een-dee-KAH-tsee-oh-nee pehr [ ]?)

Excuse me, could you show me on the map how to get to [location]?
Scusi, potrebbe indicarmi sulla mappa come arrivare a [location]?
*(SKOO-see, poh-TREB-beh een-dee-KAHR-mee SOO-lah MAHP-pah
KOH-meh ah-REE-vah-reh ah [ ]?)*

Do you know how to get to [location]?
Saprebbe come arrivare a [location]?
(SAHP-preh-beh KOH-meh ah-REE-vah-reh ah [ ]?)

I'm trying to find my way to [location]. Can you assist me?
Cerco di arrivare a [location]. Potrebbe aiutarmi?
(CHER-koh dee ah-REE-vah-reh ah [ ]. poh-TREB-beh ay-yoo-TAR-mee?)

Where can I find [location]?
Dove posso trovare [location]?
(DOH-veh POH-soh troh-VAH-reh [ ]?)

Can you direct me to [location]?
Potrebbe indicarmi la strada per [location]?
(poh-TREB-beh een-dee-KAHR-mee lah STRA-dah pehr [ ]?)

Excuse me, I'm a bit lost. Could you help me find [location]?
Mi scusi, sono un po' perso/a. potrebbe aiutarmi a trovare [location]?
*(mee SKOO-see, SOH-noh oon poh PEHR-soh/ah. poh-TREB-beh
ay-yoo-TAR-mee ah troh-VAH-reh [ ]?)*

How far is [location] from here?
Quanto dista [location] da qui?
(KWOHN-toh DEES-tah [ ] dah kwee?)

Could you tell me the quickest way to get to [location]?
Potrebbe dirmi il modo più veloce per arrivare a [location]?
*(poh-TREB-beh DEER-mee eel MOH-doh pew VEH-loh-cheh pehr
ah-REE-vah-reh ah [ ]?)*

Is it possible to walk to [location] from here?
È possibile raggiungere [location] a piedi da qui?
(eh po-SEE-beh-leh rah-JOON-geh-reh [ ] ah PYEH-dee dah kwee?)

Excuse me, do you know the way to [location]?
Mi scusi, sa dove si trova [location]?
(mee SKOO-see, sah DOH-veh see TROH-vah [ ]?)

Which is the best way to get to [location]?
Qual è il modo migliore per arrivare a [location]?
(kwahl eh eel MOH-doh MEEL-yoh-reh pehr ah-REE-vah-reh ah [ ]?)

Can you give me directions to the nearest [location]?
Potrebbe darmi le indicazioni per il [location] più vicino?
(poh-TREB-beh DAR-mee leh een-dee-KAH-tsee-oh-nee pehr eel [location] pew VEE-chi-noh?)

Excuse me, could you please repeat that?
Scusi, potrebbe ripetere per favore?
(SKOO-see, poh-TREB-beh ree-peh-TEH-reh pehr fa-VO-reh?)

Could you speak a little slower please?
Potrebbe parlare più lentamente per favore?
(poh-TREB-beh PAR-lah-reh pew len-TA-men-teh pehr fa-VO-reh?)

Sorry, I didn't understand. Could you explain it again?
Mi scusi, non ho capito. Potrebbe spiegarmelo di nuovo?
(mee SKOO-see, non oh kah-PEE-toh. poh-TREB-beh SPYEH-gar-meh-loh dee NOO-vo?)

Excuse me, where is the closest [location]?
Mi scusi, dove si trova il [location] più vicino?
(mee SKOO-see, DOH-veh see TROH-vah eel [ ] pew VEE-chi-noh?)

Can you show me on the map where [location] is?
Potrebbe indicarmi sulla mappa dove si trova [location]?
(poh-TREB-beh een-dee-KAHR-mee SOO-lah MAHP-pah DOH-veh see TROH-vah [ ]?)

Sorry to bother you, but could you tell me how to get to [location]?
Mi dispiace disturbare, ma potrebbe dirmi come arrivare a [location]?
(mee dee-SPYA-cheh dees-toor-BAH-reh, mah poh-TREB-beh DEER-mee KOH-meh ah-REE-vah-reh ah [ ]?)

Excuse me, could you recommend a good route to take to [location]?
Scusi, potrebbe consigliarmi un buon percorso per arrivare a [location]?
(SKOO-see, poh-TREB-beh kon-seel-YAR-mee oon boh-OHN per-KOR-soh pehr ah-REE-vah-reh ah [ ]?)

Could you tell me how long it takes to get to [location]?
Potrebbe dirmi quanto ci vuole per arrivare a [location]?
(poh-TREB-beh DEER-mee KWOHN-toh chee VWOH-leh pehr ah-REE-vah-reh ah [ ]?)

Excuse me, is [location] within walking distance?
Mi scusi, [location] è raggiungibile a piedi?
(mee SKOO-see, [location] eh rah-JOON-gee-bee-leh ah PYEH-dee?)

Could you tell me how to get back to [starting location]?
Potrebbe dirmi come tornare a [starting location]?
(poh-TREB-beh DEER-mee KOH-meh tohr-NAH-reh ah [starting location]?)

Excuse me, do you know any landmarks or notable places near [location]?
Mi scusi, conosce dei punti di riferimento o luoghi notevoli vicino a [location]?
(mee SKOO-see, koh-NOH-sheh dei POON-tee dee ree-feh-REE-men-toh oh loo-GHEE noh-TEH-voh-lee VEE-chee-noh ah [ ]?)

Sorry, could you speak up a little bit?
Mi scusi, potrebbe parlare un po' più forte?
(mee SKOO-see, poh-TREB-beh par-LAH-reh oon poh PEWR-teh?)

Excuse me, could you write down the directions for me please?
Mi scusi, potrebbe scrivere le indicazioni per me per favore?
(mee SKOO-see, poh-TREB-beh SKREE-veh-reh leh een-dee-KAH-tsee-oh-nee pehr meh pehr fa-VO-reh?)

Could you point me in the direction of [location]?
Potrebbe indicarmi la direzione per [location]?
(poh-TREB-beh een-dee-KAHR-mee lah dee-reh-tsee-YOH-neh pehr [ ]?)

Excuse me, do you happen to know the postcode for [location]?
Scusi, per caso conosce il codice postale di [location]?
(SKOO-see, pehr KAH-zoh koh-NOH-sheh eel KOH-dee-tcheh po-STAH-leh dee [ ]?)

Could you tell me which bus/train I need to take to get to [location]?
Potrebbe dirmi quale autobus/treno devo prendere per arrivare a [location]?
(poh-TREB-beh DEER-mee KWAH-leh AW-toh-boos/TREH-noh DEH-vo prehn-DEH-reh pehr ah-REE-vah-reh ah [ ]?)

Excuse me, is there a taxi rank nearby?
Mi scusi, c'è un parcheggio taxi qui vicino?
(mee SKOO-see, cheh oon par-KEH-joh TAH-ksee kwee VEE-chee-noh?)

Excuse me, do you know if there are any bike rental places around here?
Mi scusi, sa se ci sono dei noleggi di biciclette in zona?
(mee SKOO-see, sah seh chee SOH-noh dei noh-LE-djee dee bee-chee-KLEHT-teh een ZOH-nah?)

Could you tell me if it's safe to walk to [location] at night?
Potrebbe dirmi se è sicuro camminare per arrivare a [location] di notte?
(poh-TREB-beh DEER-mee seh eh see-KOO-roh kahm-mee-NAH-reh pehr ah-REE-vah-reh ah [location] dee NOHT-teh?)

Excuse me, could you draw me a map to [location]?
Mi scusi, potrebbe disegnarmi una mappa per arrivare a [location]?
(mee SKOO-see, poh-TREB-beh dee-SEN-yar-mee OO-nah MAH-pah pehr ah-REE-vah-reh ah [ ]?)

Excuse me, could you tell me how to get to the nearest restroom, please?
Mi scusi, potrebbe dirmi come arrivare al bagno più vicino, per favore?
(mee SKOO-see, poh-TREB-beh DEER-mee KOH-meh ah-ree-VAH-reh ahl BAH-nyoh p(y)oo VEE-chee-noh, pehr fah-VOH-reh?)

COMMON BUSINESS STATEMENTS AND QUESTIONS

Could you tell me a bit about your company's mission statement?
Puoi dirmi qualcosa sulla mission statement della tua azienda?
(pwoy DEER-mee KWAH-loh-sah SOO-nee LAH mish-ION STAYT-mehnt DEHL-lah TOO-ah ah-TSYEN-dah?)

I'm curious to know more about your core values.
Sono curioso di conoscere di più i tuoi valori fondamentali.
(SO-noh koo-ree-OH-zoh dee koh-NOH-sheh-reh dee pih-OOH EE TOO-ee VAH-loh-ree fohn-dah-MEN-tah-lee)

Can you explain your business model to me?
Puoi spiegarmi il tuo modello di business?
(pwoy SPEE-gar-mee eel TOO-oh moh-DEHL-loh dee BEE-zness?)

How does your company generate revenue?
Come fa la tua azienda a generare ricavi?
(KOH-meh fah lah TOO-ah ah-TSYEN-dah ah jeh-neh-RAH-reh ree-KAH-vee?)

Who is your target market?
Qual è il tuo mercato di riferimento?
(kwahl eh eel TOO-oh mehr-KAH-toh dee ree-feh-REN-tso?)

What sets your company apart from others in the industry?
Cosa distingue la tua azienda dalle altre del settore?
(KOH-zah dees-TEEN-gweh lah TOO-ah ah-TSYEN-dah DAHL-leh AWL-treh dehl set-TOH-reh?)

What would you say are your company's biggest strengths and weaknesses?
Quali sono, a tuo parere, i punti di forza e di debolezza della tua azienda?
(KWAH-lee SO-noh, ah TOO-oh pah-REH-reh, ee POON-tee dee FOR-tzah eh dee deh-boh-LET-tsah DEHL-lah TOO-ah ah-TSYEN-dah?)

What are your company's goals for the upcoming year?
Quali sono gli obiettivi della tua azienda per il prossimo anno?
(KWAH-lee SO-noh glee oh-BYEH-tee-vee DEHL-lah TOO-ah ah-TSYEN-dah pehr eel PROSS-ee-moh AHN-noh?)

How do you plan to measure the success of your business?
Come intendi misurare il successo della tua azienda?
(KOH-meh een-DEN-dee mee-soo-RAH-reh eel soo-CHEHS-soh DEHL-lah TOO-ah ah-TSYEN-dah?)

What are some of the biggest challenges your company has faced?
Quali sono le sfide più grandi che la tua azienda ha affrontato?
(KWAH-lee SO-noh leh SFEE-deh pee GRAHN-dee keh lah TOO-ah ah-TSYEN-dah ah ahf-FRON-tah-toh?)

Can you describe your company culture?
Puoi descrivere la cultura della tua azienda?
(pwoy deh-SKREE-veh-reh lah kool-TOO-rah DEHL-lah TOO-ah ah-TSYEN-dah?)

What are the main responsibilities of your role in the company?
Quali sono le principali responsabilità del tuo ruolo all'interno dell'azienda?
(KWAH-lee SO-noh leh preehn-chee-PAH-lee rehs-pohn-sah-bee-LEE-tah del too-oh ROO-loh ahl-LEEN-teh-roh dehl-LAH tzee-EN-dah?)

What experience do you have in this industry?
Che esperienza hai in questo settore?
(keh eh-speh-ree-EHN-tsa eye een KWEH-stoh set-TOH-reh?)

How do you handle conflicts with clients or colleagues?
Come gestisci i conflitti con clienti o colleghi?
(KOH-meh je-STEE-shee ee kohn-FLEEK-tee kon kleen-tee oh kol-LEH-ghee?)

Can you walk me through your resume and work experience?
Puoi guidarmi attraverso il tuo curriculum e la tua esperienza lavorativa?
(pwoy GWEE-dar-mee ah-trah-VES-soh eel too-oh koo-REE-kool-oom eh lah TOO-ah eh-speh-ree-EN-tsa la-VOH-ree-va?)

How do you stay updated on industry trends and developments?
Come ti aggiorni sulle tendenze e gli sviluppi del settore?
(KOH-meh tee ahd-JOR-nee sool-leh TEN-den-tseh ee yee svee-LUHP-pee del set-TOH-reh?)

What skills do you bring to the table?
Quali competenze porti sul tavolo?
(KWAH-lee kohm-peh-TEN-tseh POR-tee sool tah-VOH-loh?)

How do you prioritize tasks and manage your time effectively?
Come dai priorità alle attività e gestisci il tuo tempo in modo efficace?
(KOH-meh dai pree-oh-REE-tah ah-leh aht-tee-VEE eh je-STEE-shee eel TOO-oh TEHM-po een MOH-doh ef-fee-KAH-tcheh?)

What is your management style?
Qual è il tuo stile di gestione?
(kwahl eh eel TOO-oh STY-leh dee je-STYOH-neh?)

How do you handle pressure and tight deadlines?
Come gestisci la pressione e le scadenze stringenti?
(KOH-meh je-STEE-shee lah preh-SEE-oh-neh eh leh ska-DEN-tseh streen-JEN-tee?)

What are your long-term career goals?
Quali sono i tuoi obiettivi di carriera a lungo termine?
(KWAH-lee SO-noh ee TOO-oy oh-BYEH-tee-vee dee kahr-RYEH-rah ah LOON-goh TEHR-mee-neh?)

How do you handle constructive criticism?
Come gestisci le critiche costruttive?
(KOH-meh je-STEE-shee leh KREE-tee-keh koh-STROO-ttee-veh?)

Can you tell me about a challenging project you worked on?
Puoi parlarmi di un progetto impegnativo su cui hai lavorato?
(PWOY par-LAHR-mee dee oon proh-JET-toh eem-peh-NYA-tee-voh soo
KOO-ee eye la-VOH-rahtoh?)

How do you handle a difficult coworker?
Come affronti un collega difficile?
(KOH-meh ah-fron-TEE oon kol-LEH-gah dee-fee-CHEE-leh?)

What is your approach to problem-solving?
Qual è il tuo approccio alla risoluzione dei problemi?
(KWAH-lee eh eel TOO-oh ah-PRAW-tchoh AHL-lah
ree-soh-loo-TSYOH-neh day proh-BLEH-mee?)

What motivates you to do your best work?
Cosa ti motiva a dare il meglio sul lavoro?
(KOH-sah tee moh-TEE-vah ah DAH-reh eel MEHL-yoh sool
la-VOH-roh?)

How do you handle a mistake or failure?
Come gestisci un errore o un fallimento?
(KOH-meh je-STEE-shee oon eh-ROH-reh oh oon fahl-lee-MEN-toh?)

What are your strengths and weaknesses?
Quali sono i tuoi punti di forza e di debolezza?
(KWAH-lee SO-noh ee TOO-oy POON-tee dee FOR-tsah eh dee
deh-boh-LEHT-tsah?)

How do you stay organized and manage your workload?
Come ti mantieni organizzato e gestisci il tuo carico di lavoro?
(KOH-meh tee mahn-TYEY-nee or-gah-nee-ZAH-toh eh je-STEE-shee eel
TOO-oh kah-REE-koh dee la-VOH-roh?)

What do you know about our company and our industry?

Cosa sai della nostra azienda e del nostro settore?

(KOH-sah sah-ee DEHL-lah NOH-strah ah-ZYEN-dah eh del NOH-stroh set-TOH-reh?)

How do you handle difficult customers?

Come affronti i clienti difficili?

(KOH-meh ah-fron-TEE ee kleen-TEE dee-fee-CHEE-lee?)

What is your approach to teamwork?

Qual è il tuo approccio al lavoro di squadra?

(KWAH-lee eh eel TOO-oh ah-PRAW-tchoh ahl la-VOH-roh dee SKWAH-drah?)

What are your thoughts on company culture?

Quali sono le tue opinioni sulla cultura aziendale?

(KWAH-lee SO-noh leh TOO-eh oh-pee-NYOH-nee soo-lah KOOl-too-rah ah-tsyehn-DAH-leh?)

How do you handle multiple tasks and priorities?

Come gestisci più attività e priorità?

(KOH-meh je-STEE-shee pyoo aht-tee-VEE eh pree-oh-REE-tah-tee?)

What are your salary expectations?

Quali sono le tue aspettative di stipendio?

(KWAH-lee SO-noh leh TOO-eh ah-speht-TAH-tee-vay dee stee-PEN-dee-oh?)

How do you handle a tight deadline?

Come gestisci una scadenza stretta?

(KOH-meh je-STEE-shee oon-ah skah-DEN-tsa strett-ah?)

What are your long-term career goals?

Quali sono i tuoi obiettivi di carriera a lungo termine?

(KWAH-lee SO-noh ee TOO-oy oh-BYEHT-tee-vee dee kah-RYEH-rah ah LOON-goh TEHR-mee-neh?)

How do you handle stress in the workplace?
Come affronti lo stress sul posto di lavoro?
(KOH-meh ah-fron-TEE loh stress sool POH-stoh dee la-VOH-roh?)

What experience do you have in this field? -
Che esperienza hai in questo campo?
(keh eh-speh-ree-EHN-tsa eye een KWE-stoh KAM-poh?)

What qualities do you possess that would make you a good fit for this role? -
Quali qualità possiedi che ti rendono adatto per questo ruolo?
(KWAH-lee kwa-LIH-tah poh-SEE-eh-dee keh tee ren-DOH-noh ah-DAHT-toh pair KWE-stoh ROO-loh?)

STAYING AT A HOTEL AND BOOKING A ROOM

Hi, I'd like to book a room, please.
Ciao, vorrei prenotare una stanza, per favore.
(CHA-o, vor-REI pre-no-TA-re u-na STAN-za, per fa-VO-re)

How much is a room for one night?
Quanto costa una stanza per una notte?
(KWAN-to COS-ta u-na STAN-za per u-na NOT-te)

Do you have any availability for tonight?
Avete disponibilità per stasera?
(a-VE-te dis-poni-bi-LI-ta per sta-SE-ra)

What's the rate for a single room?
Qual è il prezzo di una camera singola?
(kwal E il PRE-tso di u-na KA-me-ra SIN-go-la)

Could you give me some information about your rooms?
Potrebbe darmi alcune informazioni sulle vostre stanze?
(po-TREB-be DAR-mi al-KU-ne in-for-ma-ZIO-ni SUL-le VOS-tre STAN-ze)

What's included in the room rate?
Cosa è incluso nel prezzo della stanza?
(KO-sa E in-CLU-so nel PRE-tso DEL-la STAN-za)

What time is check-in/check-out?
A che ora è il check-in/check-out?
(a ke O-ra E il CHEK-in/CHEK-out)

Can I get an early check-in/late check-out?
Posso fare il check-in anticipato/ritardato?
(PO-sso FA-re il CHEK-in an-ti-ci-PA-to/ri-tar-DA-to)

Is there a shuttle service to the airport?
C'è un servizio navetta per l'aeroporto?
(CE un ser-VI-zio na-VET-ta per la-E-ro-PORTO)

Can you recommend a good restaurant nearby?
Può consigliarmi un buon ristorante nelle vicinanze?
(PUO con-sig-LIAR-mi un BU-on ri-sto-RAN-te nel-LE VI-ci-NAN-ze)

Do you have room service?
Avete il servizio in camera?
(a-VE-te il ser-VI-zio in KA-me-ra)

Is there a minibar in the room?
C'è un minibar in camera?
(CE un MINI-bar in KA-me-ra)

Could I have some extra towels, please?
Potrei avere degli asciugamani extra, per favore?
(po-TREI a-VE-re dei a-SHU-ga-MA-ni EX-tra, per fa-VO-re)

Can you provide me with a map of the area?
Potrebbe fornirmi una mappa della zona?
(po-TREB-be for-NIR-mi u-na MAP-pa DEL-la ZO-na)

Is there a fitness center in the hotel?
C'è un centro fitness nell'hotel?
(CE un CEN-tro FIT-ness nel-LO-tel)

Is there a swimming pool in the hotel?
C'è una piscina nell'hotel?
(CE u-na PI-scina nel-LO-tel)

Do you provide laundry services?
Offrite servizio di lavanderia?
(of-FRI-te ser-VI-zio di la-van-DE-ria)

Is there a safe in the room?
C'è una cassaforte in camera?
(CE u-na CAS-sa-for-te in KA-me-ra)

Can I pay with a credit card?
Posso pagare con carta di credito?
(PO-sso pa-GA-re con CAR-ta di CRE-di-to)

Can I have a room with a view?
Posso avere una stanza con vista?
(PO-sso a-VE-re u-na STAN-za con VIS-ta)

What's the wifi password?
Qual è la password del wifi?
(kwal E la PAS-sword del WI-fi)

Can you recommend any local attractions?
Può consigliarmi qualche attrazione locale?
(PUO con-sig-LIAR-mi KWAL-ke a-tra-ZIO-ne LO-ca-le)

Is breakfast included in the room rate?
La colazione è inclusa nel prezzo della stanza?
(LA co-la-ZIO-ne E in-CLU-sa nel PRE-tso DEL-la STAN-za)

What time is breakfast served?
A che ora viene servita la colazione?
(a ke O-ra VIE-ne ser-VI-ta la co-la-ZIO-ne)

Do you have any parking available?
Avete parcheggio disponibile?
(a-VE-te par-KEG-gio dis-poni-BI-le)

Can you recommend a good bar in the area?
Può consigliarmi un buon bar nella zona?
(PUO con-sig-LIAR-mi un BU-on bar nel-LA ZO-na)

Can I have an extra pillow, please?
Potrei avere un cuscino extra, per favore?
(po-TREI a-VE-re un CU-sci-no EX-tra, per fa-VO-re)

What's the cancellation policy?
Qual è la politica di cancellazione?
(kwal E la po-LI-ti-ca di can-CELL-la-ZIO-ne)

Do you offer any discounts for long-term stays?
Offrite sconti per soggiorni a lungo termine?
(of-FRI-te SCON-ti per so-GIOR-ni a LUN-go TER-mi-ne)

Can I have a non-smoking room?
Posso avere una stanza per non fumatori?
(PO-sso a-VE-re u-na STAN-za per non fu-ma-TO-ri)

Can you arrange a taxi for me?
Potrebbe organizzare un taxi per me?
(po-TREB-be or-ga-NIZ-za-re un TAK-si per me)

Is there an iron and ironing board in the room?
C'è un ferro e una tavola da stiro in camera?
(CE un FER-ro e u-na TA-vo-la da STI-ro in KA-me-ra)

Can I store my luggage after check-out?
Posso lasciare i miei bagagli dopo il check-out?
(PO-sso la-SHA-re i MIEI ba-GA-li do-PO il CHEK-out)

What's the nearest subway station?
Qual è la stazione della metropolitana più vicina?
(kwal E la sta-ZIO-ne DEL-la me-tro-po-li-TA-na pio VI-ci-na)

Can you recommend a good restaurant in the area?
Può consigliarmi un buon ristorante nella zona?
(PUO con-sig-LIAR-mi un BU-on ri-sto-RAN-te nel-LA ZO-na)

Is there a fitness center or gym in the hotel?
C'è un centro fitness o palestra nell'hotel?
(CE un CEN-tro FIT-ness o pa-LES-tra nel-LO-tel)

Can I have a late check-out?
Posso fare il check-out tardi?
(PO-sso FA-re il CHEK-out TAR-di)

What's the cost for room service?
Qual è il costo per il servizio in camera?
(kwal E il CO-sto per il ser-VI-zio in KA-me-ra)

Can you call me a taxi to the airport, please?
Può chiamarmi un taxi per l'aeroporto, per favore?
(PUO ka-MAR-mi un TAK-si per LA-ero-POR-to, per fa-VO-re)

I would like to make a reservation for a single/double room.
Vorrei effettuare una prenotazione per una camera singola/doppia.
*(vor-REI ef-fet-TUA-re una pre-no-ta-ZIO-ne per U-na KA-me-ra
sin-GO-la/DOP-pia)*

THE WEATHER

What's the weather like today?
Com'è il tempo oggi?
(koh-MEH eel TEHM-poh OH-jee)

How's the weather?
Come va il tempo?
(KOH-meh vah eel TEHM-poh?)

Is it hot today?
Fa caldo oggi?
(fah KAHL-doh OH-jee?)

Is it cold outside?
Fa freddo fuori?
(fah FREH-doh FWOH-ree?)

What's the temperature outside?
Qual è la temperatura fuori?
(kwahl eh lah teh-mpeh-RAH-too-rah FWOH-ree?)

Is it raining today?
Sta piovendo oggi?
(stah pee-oh-VEN-doh OH-jee?)

Is it going to rain today?
Pioverà oggi?
(pee-oh-veh-RAH OH-jee?)

Is it going to be sunny today?
Sarà soleggiato oggi?
(sah-RAH soh-leh-JAH-toh OH-jee?)

Are we expecting snow today?
Si prevede neve oggi?
(see preh-VEH-deh NEH-veh OH-jee?)

How much snow are we expecting today?
Quanta neve ci aspettiamo oggi?
(KWAN-tah NEH-veh chee ah-speh-TEE-amoh OH-jee?)

Is it cloudy today?
È nuvoloso oggi?
(eh noo-voh-LOH-soh OH-jee?)

Is it windy today?
C'è vento oggi?
(cheh VEN-toh OH-jee?)

Is it going to be humid today?
Sarà umido oggi?
(sah-RAH oo-MEE-doh OH-jee?)

Is it going to be foggy today?
arà nebbioso oggi?
(sah-RAH nehb-bee-OH-soh OH-jee?)

Is there a chance of thunderstorms today?
C'è la possibilità di temporali oggi?
(cheh lah POH-see-bee-lee-tah dee tem-poh-RAH-lee OH-jee?)

Are we expecting hail today?
Si prevede grandine oggi?
(see preh-VEH-deh grahn-DEE-neh OH-jee?)

What's the forecast for tomorrow?
Qual è la previsione per domani?
(kwahl eh lah preh-vee-ZYOH-neh pehr doh-MAH-nee?)

What's the forecast for the weekend?
Qual è la previsione per il weekend?
(kwahl eh lah preh-vee-ZYOH-neh pehr eel WEE-kend?)

Are we expecting any weather warnings?
Ci sono avvisi meteo?
(chee SOH-noh ahv-VEE-zee MEH-teh-oh?)

Is there a chance of a tornado today?
C'è la possibilità di un tornado oggi?
(cheh lah POH-see-bee-lee-tah dee oon torn-AH-doh OH-jee?)

Is it going to be a dry day?
Sarà una giornata asciutta?
(sah-RAH oo-nah jor-NAH-tah ah-SHOO-tah?)

Is it going to be a wet day?
Sarà una giornata umida?
(sah-RAH oo-nah jor-NAH-tah oo-MEE-dah?)

What's the humidity level today?
Qual è il livello di umidità oggi?
(kwahl eh eel LEE-vehl-loh dee oo-mee-DEE-tah OH-jee?)

Is there a chance of a heatwave?
C'è la possibilità di una ondata di calore?
(cheh lah poh-see-bee-LEE-tah dee oo-nah ohn-DAH-tah dee kah-LOH-reh?)

Is it going to be a muggy day?
Sarà una giornata afosa?
(sah-RAH oo-nah jor-NAH-tah ah-FOH-sah?)

Is it going to be a breezy day?
Sarà una giornata ventilata?
(sah-RAH oo-nah jor-NAH-tah ven-tee-LAH-tah?)

Is it going to be a calm day?
Sarà una giornata tranquilla?
(sah-RAH oo-nah jor-NAH-tah trahn-KWEE-lah?)

Is it going to be a stormy day?
Sarà una giornata tempestosa?
(sah-RAH oo-nah jor-NAH-tah tem-peh-STOH-sah?)

Is there a chance of thunderstorms tonight?
C'è la possibilità di temporali stasera?
(cheh lah poh-see-bee-LEE-tah dee tem-poh-RAH-lee stah-SEH-rah?)

What's the weather forecast for the week?
Qual è la previsione meteo per la settimana?
(kwahl eh lah preh-vee-ZYOH-neh MEH-teh-oh pehr lah set-tee-MAH-nah?)

Is it going to be a windy week?
Sarà una settimana ventosa?
(sah-RAH oo-nah set-tee-MAH-nah ven-TOH-sah?)

Is it going to be a snowy week?
Sarà una settimana nevosa?
(sah-RAH oo-nah set-tee-MAH-nah neh-VOH-sah?)

Is it going to be a hot week?
Sarà una settimana calda?
(sah-RAH oo-nah set-tee-MAH-nah KAHL-dah?)

Is it going to be a cold week?
Sarà una settimana fredda?
(sah-RAH oo-nah set-tee-MAH-nah FREH-dah?)

What's the weather forecast for the month?
Qual è la previsione meteo per il mese?
(kwahl eh lah preh-vee-ZYOH-neh MEH-teh-oh pehr eel MEH-zeh?)

Is it going to be a rainy month?
Sarà un mese piovoso?
(sah-RAH oon MEH-zeh pee-oh-VOH-soh?)

Is it going to be a sunny month?
Sarà un mese soleggiato?
(sah-RAH oon MEH-zeh soh-leh-JAH-toh?)

Is it going to bea humid month?
Sarà un mese umido?
(sah-RAH oon MEH-zeh oo-MEE-doh?)

Is it going to be a dry month?
Sarà un mese secco?
(sah-RAH oon MEH-zeh SEK-koh?)

Is there a chance of snow this month?
C'è la possibilità di neve questo mese?
(cheh lah poh-see-bee-LEE-tah dee NEH-veh KWEH-stoh MEH-zeh?)

WORKING OUT AT A GYM

What are your hours of operation?
Che ore siete aperti?
(keh O-reh SYEH-teh ah-PEHR-tee)

Do you offer personal training?
Offrite corsi di allenamento personale?
(oh-FREE-teh KOR-see dee ah-lleh-nah-MEN-toh pehr-soh-NAH-leh)

How much does a membership cost?
Quanto costa l'iscrizione?
(KWAN-toh KOS-tah lees-KREE-tsyoh-neh)

Are there any discounts available?
Ci sono sconti disponibili?
(chee SOH-noh SKON-tee dee-speh-NEE-bee-lee)

What types of equipment do you have?
Che tipo di attrezzatura avete?
(keh TEE-po dee aht-treh-tzoo-RAH-too-rah AH-veh-teh)

How busy is the gym usually?
Quanto è affollata la palestra di solito?
(KWAN-toh eh af-fohl-LAH-tah lah pah-LEH-strah dee soh-LEE-toh)

Do you have a sauna or steam room?
Avete una sauna o bagno turco?
(ah-VEH-teh OO-nah SAO-nah oh BAH-nyoh TOOR-koh)

Are there any classes available?
Ci sono corsi disponibili?
(chee SOH-noh KOR-see dee-speh-NEE-bee-lee)

Can I try the gym before signing up?
Posso provare la palestra prima di iscrivermi?
*(POHs-soh proh-VAH-reh lah pah-LEH-strah PREE-mah dee
ees-KREE-vehr-mee)*

Do you have lockers available?
Avete armadietti disponibili?
(ah-VEH-teh ar-mah-DYEH-tee dee-speh-NEE-bee-lee)

How often do you clean the equipment?
Con quale frequenza pulite l'attrezzatura?
*(kohn KWAH-leh freh-KWEN-tsa poo-LEE-teh
laht-treh-tzoo-RAH-too-rah)*

Is there a dress code?
C'è un codice di abbigliamento?
(cheh oon KOH-dee-tseh dee ahb-bee-LYEH-men-toh)

Do you offer towel service?
Offrite il servizio di asciugamani?
(oh-FREE-teh eel sehr-VEE-tsyoh dee ah-SHOO-gah-mah-nee)

Are there any restrictions on gym use?
Ci sono restrizioni sull'uso della palestra?
*(chee SOH-noh rehs-tree-ZYO-nee sool-LOO-zoh DEHL-lah
pah-LEH-strah)*

How many locations do you have?
Quanti centri fitness avete?
(KWAN-tee CHEN-tree FEE-tnes AH-veh-teh)

Can I bring a friend to the gym?
Posso portare un amico in palestra?
(POHs-soh pohr-TAH-reh oon ah-MEE-koh een pah-LEH-strah)

What are the busiest times of day?
Quali sono gli orari più affollati della giornata?
*(KWAL-ee SOH-noh joh-RAH-ree pyoo af-foh-LAH-tee dahl-lah
jor-NAH-tah)*

Are there any age restrictions for using the gym?
Ci sono limiti d'età per utilizzare la palestra?
(chee SOH-noh LEE-mee-tee DEH-tah pehr oo-tee-leez-ZAH-reh lah pah-LEH-strah)

Do you offer childcare services?
Offrite servizi di assistenza ai bambini?
(oh-FREE-teh sehr-VEE-tsee dee ah-see-STEN-tsa ah-ee bahm-BEE-nee)

Is there a cancellation policy?
C'è una politica di cancellazione?
(cheh EH OO-nah poh-LEE-tee-kah dee kahn-cheh-LAHT-see-yoh-neh)

Do you offer nutrition services?
Offrite servizi nutrizionali?
(oh-FREE-teh sehr-VEE-tsee noo-tree-tsyoh-NAH-lee)

Do you have a pool?
Avete una piscina?
(ah-VEH-teh OO-nah pee-SHEE-nah)

Do you offer any fitness challenges or programs?
Offrite sfide o programmi di fitness?
(oh-FREE-teh SFEED-deh oh proh-GRAHM-mee dee FEE-tnes)

Can I use the gym if I'm not a member?
Posso usare la palestra anche se non sono un membro?
(POHs-soh oo-SAH-reh lah pah-LEH-strah AHN-keh seh non SOH-noh oon MEM-broh)

What are your personal training rates?
Quali sono i vostri prezzi per il personal training?
(KWAL-ee SOH-noh ee VOHS-tree PREHT-tsee pehr eel pehr-soh-nahl tray-NEEN)

Do you have Wi-Fi available?
Avete Wi-Fi disponibile?
(ah-VEH-teh WEE-FEE dee-speh-NEE-bee-lee)

What types of weights do you have?
Che tipi di pesi avete?
(keh TEE-pee dee PEH-zee AH-veh-teh)

Are there any classes specifically for beginners?
Ci sono corsi specifici per principianti?
*(chee SOH-noh KOR-see speh-SEE-fee-chee pehr
pree-tchee-pee-AHN-tee)*

Do you offer any discounts for long-term memberships?
Offrite sconti per l'iscrizione a lungo termine?
*(oh-FREE-teh SKON-tee pehr lees-KREE-tsyoh-neh ah LOON-goh
TEHR-mee-neh)*

Is there a limit to how long I can use the gym?
C'è un limite di tempo per l'uso della palestra?
*(cheh eh oon LEE-mee-teh dee TEHM-poh pehr loo-zoh DEHL-lah
pah-LEH-strah)*

Are there any group fitness classes?
Ci sono corsi di fitness di gruppo?
(chee SOH-noh KOR-see dee FEE-tnes dee GROOP-po)

Do you have a membership referral program?
Avete un programma di referenze per l'iscrizione?
*(ah-VEH-teh oon proh-GRAHM-mah dee reh-FEH-rehn-tseh pehr
lees-KREE-tsyoh-neh)*

Are there any additional fees besides the membership fee?
Ci sono spese aggiuntive oltre alla quota di iscrizione?
*(chee SOH-noh SPEH-zeh ahd-JOON-dee-teev-eh OHL-treh AHL-lah
KOH-tah dee lees-KREE-tsyoh-neh)*

Do you offer personal lockers for storing items?
Offrite armadietti personali per riporre gli oggetti?
*(oh-FREE-teh ahr-mah-DYEH-tee pehr-soh-NAH-lee pehr ree-POHR-reh
lyee ohb-JEHT-tee)*

Can I bring a guest with me to the gym?
Posso portare un ospite con me in palestra?
*(POHs-soh pohr-TAH-reh oon oh-SPEE-teh kohn meh een
pah-LEH-strah)*

Do you provide towels for members to use?
Fornite gli asciugamani per l'uso dei membri?
(for-NEE-teh lyee ah-SYOO-gah-mah-nee pehr loo-soh day MEM-bree)

Is there a dress code?
C'è un codice di abbigliamento?
(cheh eh oon KOH-dee-tcheh dee ahb-bee-LYAH-men-toh)

Do you have a sauna or steam room?
Avete una sauna o una stanza del vapore?
(ah-VEH-teh OO-nah SOW-nah oh OO-nah STAN-tsa dehl VAH-poh-reh)

Are there any discounts for students or seniors?
Ci sono sconti per studenti o anziani?
(chee SOH-noh SKON-tee pehr stoo-DEHN-tee oh ahn-TSYAH-nee)

**I need help using the equipment. Can you show me how to use it
properly?**
Ho bisogno di aiuto nell'utilizzo delle attrezzature. Puoi mostrarmi
come usarle correttamente?
*(oh bee-ZOH-nyoh dee ah-YOO-toh nell-oo-tee-LEE-zoh DEHL-leh
ah-treh-TSAH-too-reh. PWOY mohs-TRAHR-mee KOH-meh oo-ZAHR-leh
kohr-REHT-teh-mehn-teh)*

TALKING TO A PHYSICIAN

Hello, doctor.
Buongiorno, dottore.
(BWOHN-johr-noh, DOHT-toh-reh)

Nice to meet you.
Piacere di conoscerla.
(pyah-CHAY-reh dee koh-NOH-shehr-lah)

Thank you for seeing me today.
Grazie per avermi visitato oggi.
(GRAH-tsyeh pehr ah-VEHR-mee vee-ZEE-tah-toh OHG-ghee)

I have an appointment with you.
Ho un appuntamento con lei.
(oh oon ah-poon-tah-MEHN-toh kohn lay)

I'm here to discuss my health concerns with you.
Sono qui per discutere dei miei problemi di salute con lei.
*(SOH-noh kwee pehr dee-SKOO-teh-reh dey MEE-eh proh-BLEH-mee
dee sahl-OOT-teh kohn lay)*

I'm not feeling well.
Non mi sento bene.
(nohn mee SEHN-toh BEH-neh)

I'm experiencing some health problems.
Sto avendo dei problemi di salute.
(stoh ah-VEHN-doh dey proh-BLEH-mee dee sahl-OOT-teh)

I need your advice regarding my health.
Ho bisogno del suo consiglio per quanto riguarda la mia salute.
*(oh bee-SOH-nyoh dehl SWOH kohn-SEE-lyoh pehr KWAN-toh
ree-GWAHR-dah lah MEE-ah sahl-OOT-teh)*

Can you help me with my health issues?
Mi può aiutare con i miei problemi di salute?
(mee PWOH ah-yoo-TAH-reh kohn ee MEE-eh proh-BLEH-mee dee sahl-OOT-teh?)

What do you recommend for my current health condition?
Cosa mi consiglia per la mia condizione di salute attuale?
(KOH-sah mee kohn-SEEL-yah pehr lah MEE-ah kohn-dee-TSYOH-neh dee sahl-OOT-teh ah-TOO-eh-leh?)

I have some questions about my health.
Ho alcune domande sulla mia salute.
(oh ahl-KOO-neh doh-MAHN-deh SOO-lah lah MEE-ah sahl-OOT-teh)

Can you explain my diagnosis to me?
Mi può spiegare la mia diagnosi?
(mee PWOH spyah-GAH-reh lah MEE-ah dee-NAH-goh-zee?)

What tests do I need to undergo?
Quali esami devo sottopormi?
(KWAH-lee eh-ZAH-mee DEH-voh SOHT-toh-POHR-mee?)

Can you prescribe me some medication?
Mi può prescrivere qualche medicinale?
(mee PWOH preh-SKREE-veh-reh KWAHL-keh meh-dee-CHEE-nah-leh?)

How long will it take for me to recover?
 Quanto tempo ci vorrà per riprendermi?
(KWAN-toh TEHM-poh chee vohr-RAH pehr ree-prehn-DEHR-mee?)

Can you provide me with a referral?
Mi può fornire un rinvio?
(mee PWOH fohr-NEE-reh oon REEN-vee-yoh?)

I'm allergic to certain medications.
Sono allergico a certi medicinali.
(SOH-noh ah-lleh-RJEE-koh ah CHEHR-tee meh-dee-chee-NAH-lee)

I'm taking medication for another condition.
Sto prendendo dei medicinali per un'altra condizione.
(stoh prehn-DEHN-doh dey meh-dee-chee-NAH-lee pehr oon-AHL-troh kohn-dee-TSYOH-neh)

I have a history of medical problems in my family.
Ho una storia di problemi di salute nella mia famiglia.
(oh OO-nah STOH-ryah dee proh-BLEH-mee dee sahl-OOT-teh NEHL-lah MEE-ah fah-MEE-lyah)

Can you recommend a specialist for my condition?
Può consigliarmi uno specialista per la mia condizione?
(PWOH kohn-SEELYAHR-mee OO-noh speh-chee-LIS-tah pehr lah MEE-ah kohn-dee-TSYOH-neh?)

What lifestyle changes do I need to make for my health?
Quali cambiamenti del mio stile di vita devo fare per la mia salute?
(KWAH-lee kahm-BYAH-mehn-tee dehl MEE-oh STEE-leh dee VEE-tah DEH-voh FAH-reh pehr lah MEE-ah sahl-OOT-teh?)

How often should I come in for check-ups?
Con quale frequenza dovrei fare controlli medici?
(kohn KWAH-leh freh-KWEN-tsah DOH-vreh fah-reh kohn-TROHL-lee MEH-dee-chee?)

Can you explain the side effects of this medication?
Può spiegarmi gli effetti collaterali di questo medicinale?
(PWOH spyah-GAH-reh-mee glee eh-FEH-tee koh-lah-teh-RAH-lee dee KWEH-stoh meh-dee-chee-NAH-leh?)

I have trouble sleeping at night.
Ho difficoltà a dormire di notte.
(oh dee-fee-KOHL-tah ah dohr-MEE-reh dee NOHT-teh)

I have a persistent cough.
Ho una tosse persistente.
(oh OO-nah TOH-sseh pehr-see-STEHN-teh)

I have a fever.
Ho la febbre.
(oh lah FEHB-breh)

I'm experiencing chest pain.
Sto avendo dolore al petto.
(stoh ah-VEHN-doh DOH-loh-reh ahl PEHT-toh)

I have a headache.
Ho mal di testa.
(oh mahl dee TEH-stah)

I feel dizzy.
Ho le vertigini.
(oh leh vehr-tee-JEE-nee)

I feel nauseous.
Ho la nausea.
(oh lah nah-OH-zah)

I have diarrhea.
Ho la diarrea.
(oh lah dee-ah-RREH-ah)

Is there anything I need to avoid while taking this medication?
C'è qualcosa che devo evitare mentre assumo questo farmaco?
*(chay KWOHL-koh keh DOH-voh eh-vee-TAH-reh MEHN-treh
ah-SOO-moh KWES-toh FAR-ma-ko?)*

**Can you tell me more about the surgeryprocedure I need to
undergo?**
Puoi darmi maggiori informazioni sulla chirurgiaprocedura a cui devo
sottopormi?
*(pwoy DAHR-mee mahd-JOH-ree een-fohr-ma-TSYOH-nee SOO-lah
kee-roor-JEE-ahproh-tcheh-DOO-rah ah KOO-ee DEH-voh
soht-toh-POHR-mee?)*

85

How long will it take for me to recover from the surgeryprocedure?
Quanto tempo ci vorrà per riprendermi dalla chirurgia/procedura?
*(KWAN-toh TEM-poh chee VOHR-rah pehr ree-prehn-DEHR-mee
DAH-lah kee-roor-JEE-ah/proh-tcheh-DOO-rah?)*

**What are the potential risks and complications of the
surgery/procedure?**
Quali sono i rischi potenziali e le complicanze della
chirurgia/procedura?
*(KWAH-lee SOH-noh ee REES-kee poh-TEN-tsee-AH-lee eh leh
kohm-plee-KAHN-tseh DEHL-lah
kee-roor-JEE-ah/proh-tcheh-DOO-rah?)*

Can you recommend any support groups for my condition?
Puoi consigliarmi qualche gruppo di sostegno per la mia condizione?
*(pwoy kohn-see-LYAR-mee KWAHL-keh GROOP-poh dee
sohs-TEHN-yoh pehr lah MEE-ah kohn-dee-TSYOH-neh?)*

What should I do if I experience any complications or side effects?
Cosa devo fare se riscontro complicazioni o effetti collaterali?
*(KOH-sah DEH-voh FAH-reh seh ree-STROH kohm-plee-kah-TSYOH-nee
oh eh-FEH-tee koh-lah-teh-RAH-lee?)*

Can you provide me with a medical certificate for my employer?
Puoi fornirmi un certificato medico per il mio datore di lavoro?
*(pwoy fohr-NEER-mee oon cher-tee-fee-KAH-toh MEH-dee-koh pehr eel
MEE-oh dah-TOH-reh dee lah-VOH-roh?)*

Can you help me fill out my insurance claim forms?
Puoi aiutarmi a compilare i moduli di richiesta di assicurazione?
*(pwoy ah-yoo-TAHR-mee ah kohm-pee-LAH-reh ee MOH-doo-lee dee
ree-KEY-stah dee ah-ssee-koo-rah-TSYOH-neh?)*

Thank you for your time and expertise.
Grazie per il tuo tempo e la tua competenza.
*(GRAH-tsyeh pehr eel TOO-oh TEHM-poh eh lah TOO-ah
kohm-peh-TEN-tsyah.)*

MAKING A MEDICAL APPOINTMENT

Hello, I would like to schedule an appointment with a doctor.
Ciao, Vorrei fissare un appuntamento con un medico.
(chow, vor-RAY fee-SAH-reh oon ah-poon-ta-MEN-toh kon oon MEH-dee-koh)

Can I make an appointment to see the doctor, please?
Posso fissare un appuntamento per vedere il medico, per favore?
(POH-soh fee-SAH-reh oon ah-poon-ta-MEN-toh pehr veh-DEH-reh eel MEH-dee-koh, pehr fa-VOH-reh)

I need to see a doctor as soon as possible.
Ho bisogno di vedere un medico il prima possibile.
(oh bee-ZOHN-doh dee veh-DEH-reh oon MEH-dee-koh eel pree-MAH po-SEE-beh-leh)

Can you please help me schedule an appointment with a specialist?
Può aiutarmi a fissare un appuntamento con uno specialista, per favore?
(pwOH ah-yoo-TAHR-mee ah fee-SAH-reh oon ah-poon-ta-MEN-toh kon oo-no speh-chee-AL-ista, pehr fa-VOH-reh)

I need to make an appointment for a physical examination.
Devo fissare un appuntamento per un esame fisico.
(DEH-voh fee-SAH-reh oon ah-poon-ta-MEN-toh pehr oon eh-ZAH-meh FEE-see-koh)

I'm experiencing some health issues and would like to see a doctor.
Ho dei problemi di salute e vorrei vedere un medico.
(oh dei proh-BLEH-mee dee sahl-OOT-eh eh vor-RAY veh-DEH-reh oon MEH-dee-koh)

I would like to book an appointment for my child to see a pediatrician.
Vorrei prenotare un appuntamento per mio figlio/a per vedere un pediatra.
(vor-RAY preh-noh-TAH-reh oon ah-poon-ta-MEN-toh pehr MEE-oh FEE-lyoh/ah pehr veh-DEH-reh oon peh-dee-AH-trah)

Can you tell me the soonest available appointment?
Mi può dire il primo appuntamento disponibile?
(mee pwoh DEE-reh eel PREE-stoh ah-poon-ta-MEN-toh dees-poh-NEE-beh-leh)

Is it possible to schedule an appointment for today?
È possibile fissare un appuntamento per oggi?
(eh pos-SEE-beh-leh fee-SAH-reh oon ah-poon-ta-MEN-toh pehr OH-djee)

Do you have any appointments available this week?
Ha degli appuntamenti disponibili questa settimana?
(ah DEH-lee ah-poon-ta-MEN-tee dees-poh-NEE-bee-lee kwes-tah set-TEE-mah-nah)

How long will the appointment take?
Quanto tempo durerà l'appuntamento?
(KWAN-toh TEM-po doo-REH-rah lah-poon-ta-MEN-toh)

Can I cancel or reschedule my appointment?
Posso cancellare o ri-programmare l'appuntamento?
(POH-soh kahn-cheh-LAH-reh oh ree-proh-GRAHM-mah-reh lah-poon-ta-MEN-toh)

I need to change my appointment time.
Devo cambiare l'orario dell'appuntamento.
(DEH-voh kahm-BYAH-reh loh-RAH-ree-oh del-lah-poon-ta-MEN-toh)

I won't be able to make it to my appointment.
Non potrò venire all'appuntamento.
(non po-TRAW veh-NEE-reh ahl-lah-poon-ta-MEN-toh)

I would like to see a specific doctor.
Vorrei vedere un medico specifico.
(vor-RAY veh-DEH-reh oon MEH-dee-koh speh-SEE-fee-koh)

Can I schedule a virtual appointment?
Posso fissare un appuntamento virtuale?
(POH-soh fee-SAH-reh oon ah-poon-ta-MEN-toh veer-too-AH-leh)

Do I need to bring any paperwork or documents to my appointment?
Devo portare dei documenti o delle carte all'appuntamento?
*(DEH-voh pohr-TAH-reh dei do-koo-MEN-tee oh DEHL-leh KAR-teh
ahl-lah-poon-ta-MEN-toh)*

What do I need to bring with me to my appointment?
Cosa devo portare con me all'appuntamento?
(KOH-sah DEH-voh pohr-TAH-reh kohn meh ahl-lah-poon-ta-MEN-toh)

Can I bring a friend or family member to my appointment?
Posso portare un amico o un familiare all'appuntamento?
*(POH-soh pohr-TAH-reh oon ah-MEE-koh oh oon fah-MEE-lyah-reh
ahl-lah-poon-ta-MEN-toh)*

How much will the appointment cost?
Quanto costa l'appuntamento?
(KWAN-toh KOH-stah lah-poon-ta-MEN-toh)

Do you accept my insurance?
Accettate la mia assicurazione?
(ah-chet-TAH-teh lah MEE-ah ah-ssee-koo-rah-tsyoh-neh)

Is there a copay or deductible for the appointment?
C'è una quota a carico o una franchigia per l'appuntamento?
*(cheh OO-nah KWOH-tah ah KAH-ree-koh oh OO-nah frahn-KEE-jah
pehr lah-poon-ta-MEN-toh)*

When is the earliest appointment available?
Quando è disponibile il primo appuntamento?
*(KWAN-doh eh dees-poh-NEE-beh-leh eel PREE-stoh
ah-poon-ta-MEN-toh)*

Can I request a same-day appointment?
Posso richiedere un appuntamento per lo stesso giorno?
(POH-soh ree-kyeh-DEH-reh oon ah-poon-ta-MEN-toh pehr loh SAHM-meh JOHR-noh)

Can I schedule an appointment for next week?
Posso fissare un appuntamento per la prossima settimana?
(POH-soh fee-SAH-reh oon ah-poon-ta-MEN-toh pehr lah PROHS-see-mah seh-ttee-MAH-nah)

Can I schedule an appointment for next month?
Posso fissare un appuntamento per il prossimo mese?
(POH-soh fee-SAH-reh oon ah-poon-ta-MEN-toh pehr eel PROHS-see-moh MEH-zeh)

Can you remind me of my appointment date and time?
Può ricordarmi la data e l'ora del mio appuntamento?
(pwòh ree-kor-DAR-mee lah DAH-tah eh LOH-rah del mèe-oh ah-poon-ta-MEN-toh)

Can I make an appointment for a specific time?
Posso fare un appuntamento per un orario specifico?
(POH-soh FAH-reh oon ah-poon-ta-MEN-toh pehr oon oh-RAH-ree-oh speh-SEE-fee-koh)

Can I book an appointment online?
Posso prenotare un appuntamento online?
(POH-soh preh-noh-TAH-reh oon ah-poon-ta-MEN-toh on-LINE)

Can I book an appointment over the phone?
Posso prenotare un appuntamento telefonicamente?
(POH-soh preh-noh-TAH-reh oon ah-poon-ta-MEN-toh teh-leh-foh-nee-KAH-mehn-teh)

Can you recommend a doctor for me?
Può consigliarmi un medico?
(pwòh kon-see-LYAR-mee oon MEH-dee-koh)

Can I see the same doctor for follow-up appointments?
Posso vedere lo stesso medico per i successivi appuntamenti?
(POH-soh veh-DEH-reh loh STESS-soh MEH-dee-koh pehr ee
soo-KSESS-see-vee ah-poon-ta-MEN-tee)

Can I schedule regular appointments in advance?
Posso fissare degli appuntamenti regolari in anticipo?
(POH-soh fee-SAH-reh DEH-yee ah-poon-ta-MEN-tee reh-GOH-lah-ree
een ahn-TEE-chee-poh)

Can I get a reminder call before my appointment?
Posso ricevere una chiamata di promemoria prima del mio
appuntamento?
(POH-soh ree-CHEH-veh-reh OO-nah kyah-MAH-tah dee
proh-meh-MOH-ree-ah PREE-mah del mèe-oh ah-poon-ta-MEN-toh)

Can I reschedule my appointment?
Posso cambiare la data del mio appuntamento?
(POH-soh kahm-BYAH-reh lah DAH-tah del mèe-oh
ah-poon-ta-MEN-toh)

Can I cancel my appointment?
Posso annullare il mio appuntamento?
(POH-soh ahn-nool-LAH-reh eel mèe-oh ah-poon-ta-MEN-toh)

Is there anything I need to bring to my appointment?
C'è qualcosa che devo portare al mio appuntamento?
(CHEH kwahl-KOH-zah keh DEH-voh pohr-TAH-reh ahl mèe-oh
ah-poon-ta-MEN-toh?)

How much will my appointment cost?
Quanto costerà il mio appuntamento?
(KWAN-toh koh-steh-RÀ eel MÈE-oh ah-poon-ta-MEN-toh?)

Can you remind me of the date and time of my appointment?
Puoi ricordarmi la data e l'ora del mio appuntamento?
(PWOH-ee ree-kor-DAHR-mee lah DAH-tah eh LOH-rah del mèe-oh
ah-poon-ta-MEN-toh?)

Can I have a copy of my medical records?
Posso avere una copia delle mie cartelle cliniche?
(POH-soh ah-VEH-reh OO-nah KOH-pyah DEHL-leh MEE-eh kar-TEL-leh
KLEE-nee-keh?)

TALKING TO A DENTIST

Can you tell me about your dental practice?
Posso sapere qualcosa sulla sua pratica dentale?
(POSSO sa-PE-re kwa-LCO-sa SUL-la SUA pra-TI-ca DEN-ta-le)

What services do you offer?
Quali servizi offrite?
(QUA-li ser-VI-zi of-FRI-te)

How often should I have a dental check-up?
Quanto spesso dovrei fare il controllo dentale?
(QUAN-to SPE-sso do-VRE-i FA-re il con-TROL-lo DEN-ta-le)

Do you have experience treating patients with dental anxiety?
Avete esperienza nel trattamento dei pazienti con ansia dentale?
(A-ve-te es-pe-RI-en-za nel trat-ta-MEN-to dei pa-ZIEN-ti con AN-sia den-TA-le)

How do you handle dental emergencies?
Come gestite le emergenze dentali?
(CO-me GE-sti-te le e-MER-gen-ze den-TA-li)

Can you explain the dental treatment options available to me?
Potrebbe spiegarmi le opzioni di trattamento dentale disponibili?
(POT-reb-be SPIE-gar-mi le OP-zio-ni di trat-ta-MEN-to DEN-ta-le di-SPO-ni-bi-li)

What is your approach to preventive dental care?
Qual è il vostro approccio alla cura dentale preventiva?
(QUAL è il VOS-tro a-PROC-cio al-la CU-ra den-TA-le pre-ven-TI-va)

Do you offer cosmetic dentistry services?
Offrite servizi di odontoiatria estetica?
(OF-fri-te ser-VI-zi di o-don-toi-A-tria e-STET-ti-ca)

How can I improve my dental hygiene at home?
Come posso migliorare la mia igiene dentale a casa?
(CO-me POSSO mi-glio-RA-re la MIA i-GE-ne DEN-ta-le a CA-sa)

How often should I replace my toothbrush?
Quanto spesso dovrei sostituire lo spazzolino da denti?
(QUAN-to SPE-sso do-VRE-i sos-ti-TUI-re lo SPA-zzo-li-no da DEN-ti)

Do you recommend using mouthwash?
Mi consigliate di usare il collutorio?
(Mi con-sig-LIA-te di u-SA-re il col-lu-TO-rio)

Can you tell me about the benefits of fluoride?
Potete parlarmi dei benefici del fluoro?
(Po-TE-te par-LAR-mi DEI be-NE-fi-ci del FLUO-ro)

How can I prevent cavities?
Come posso prevenire le carie?
(CO-me POSSO pre-ve-NI-re le CA-rie)

Can you explain the process of getting a dental filling?
Potete spiegarmi il processo per ottenere una otturazione dentale?
*(Po-TE-te spie-GAR-mi il pro-CES-so per ot-te-NE-re U-na
ot-tu-RA-zio-ne den-TA-le)*

What are the benefits of dental crowns?
Quali sono i vantaggi delle corone dentali?
(QUA-li SO-no i VAN-ta-ggi DEL-le CO-ro-ne den-TA-li)

How can I fix crooked or misaligned teeth?
Come posso correggere denti storti o malallineati?
(CO-me POSSO cor-RE-ge-re DEN-ti STOR-ti o ma-la-lli-NE-a-ti)

Do you offer orthodontic treatments?
Offrite trattamenti ortodontici?
(OF-fri-te trat-ta-MEN-ti or-to-DON-ti-ci)

How can I treat gum disease?
Come posso trattare la malattia gengivale?
(CO-me POSSO trat-TA-re la ma-LAT-tia gen-GI-va-le)

What causes bad breath and how can I prevent it?
Cosa causa il cattivo alito e come posso prevenirlo?
(CO-sa CAU-sa il cat-TI-vo A-li-to e CO-me POSSO pre-ve-NIR-lo)

Can you explain the process of getting a dental implant?
Potete spiegarmi il processo per ottenere un impianto dentale?
(Po-TE-te spie-GAR-mi il pro-CES-so per ot-te-NE-re un im-PIAN-to den-TA-le)

What are the benefits of dental implants?
Quali sono i vantaggi degli impianti dentali?
(QUA-li SO-no i VAN-ta-ggi DE-gli im-PIAN-ti den-TA-li)

How can I whiten my teeth?
Come posso sbiancare i denti?
(CO-me POSSO sbian-CARE i DEN-ti)

Do you offer teeth whitening treatments?
Offrite trattamenti per sbiancare i denti?
(OF-fri-te trat-ta-MEN-ti per sbian-CARE i DEN-ti)

Can you explain the different types of dental bridges?
Potete spiegarmi i diversi tipi di ponti dentali?
(Po-TE-te spie-GAR-mi i di-VER-si TI-pi di PON-ti den-TA-li)

How can I care for my dental implants?
Come posso prendere cura dei miei impianti dentali?
(CO-me POSSO pren-DE-re CU-ra DEI MIE-i im-PIAN-ti den-TA-li)

Can you explain the different types of dental veneers?
Potete spiegarmi i diversi tipi di faccette dentali?
(Po-TE-te spie-GAR-mi i di-VER-si TI-pi di fa-CET-te den-TA-li)

What are the benefits of dental veneers?
Quali sono i vantaggi delle faccette dentali?
(QUA-li SO-no i VAN-ta-ggi DEL-le fa-CET-te den-TA-li)

How can I prevent teeth grinding?
Come posso prevenire il digrignamento dei denti?
(CO-me POSSO pre-ve-NI-re il di-GRI-gna-MEN-to DEI DEN-ti)

Can you explain the process of getting a dental crown?
Potete spiegarmi il processo per ottenere una corona dentale?
(Po-TE-te spie-GAR-mi il pro-CES-so per ot-te-NE-re U-na CO-ro-na den-TA-le)

What are the benefits of dental bonding?
Quali sono i vantaggi del bonding dentale?
(QUA-li SO-no i VAN-ta-ggi del BON-ding den-TA-le)

Can you explain the process of getting a dental filling?
Potete spiegarmi il processo per ottenere una otturazione dentale?
(Po-TE-te spie-GAR-mi il pro-CES-so per ot-te-NE-re U-na ot-tu-ra-ZIO-ne den-TA-le)

What are the different types of dental fillings available?
Quali sono i diversi tipi di otturazioni dentali disponibili?
(QUA-li SO-no i di-VER-si TI-pi di ot-tu-ra-ZIO-ni den-TA-li dis-po-NI-bi-li)

How often should I visit the dentist for a check-up?
Quanto spesso dovrei fare un controllo dal dentista?
(QUAN-to SPES-so DO-vrei FA-re un con-TROL-lo dal den-TI-sta)

What can I expect during a dental check-up?
Cosa posso aspettarmi durante un controllo dal dentista?
(CO-sa POSSO as-PET-tar-mi DU-ran-te un con-TROL-lo dal den-TI-sta)

Can you recommend any ways to relieve dental pain?
Potete consigliare dei modi per alleviare il dolore dentale?
(Po-TE-te con-SIGLIA-re dei MO-di per al-le-VIA-re il DO-lo-re den-TA-le)

How can I maintain good oral hygiene?
Come posso mantenere una buona igiene orale?
(CO-me POSSO man-TE-ne-re U-na BUA-na i-GIE-ne o-RA-le)

Can you explain the process of getting a dental extraction?
Potete spiegarmi il processo per ottenere un'estrazione dentale?
(Po-TE-te spie-GAR-mi il pro-CES-so per ot-te-NE-re un'ES-tra-ZIO-ne den-TA-le)

What are the benefits of regular teeth cleanings?
Quali sono i vantaggi delle pulizie dei denti regolari?
(QUA-li SO-no i VAN-ta-ggi DEL-le pu-LI-zie DEI DEN-ti re-go-LA-ri)

Can you explain the difference between a root canal and a dental filling?
Potete spiegare la differenza tra un trattamento canalare e una otturazione dentale?
(Po-TE-te spi-GA-re la dif-fe-REN-za tra un trat-ta-MEN-to ca-na-LA-re e U-na ot-tu-ra-ZIO-ne den-TA-le)

What are the common causes of tooth sensitivity and how can I treat it?
Quali sono le cause comuni della sensibilità dentale e come posso trattarla?
(QUA-li SO-no le CAU-se CO-mu-NI DEL-la sen-si-bi-li-TÀ den-TA-le e CO-me POSSO trat-TAR-la)

COMMON GREETINGS

Hello
Ciao
(chow)

Hi
Salve
(SAHL-veh)

Hey
Ehi
(EH-ee)

Good morning
Buongiorno
(BWOHN-jor-noh)

Good afternoon
Buon pomeriggio
(BWOHN poh-meh-REE-joh)

Good evening
Buona sera
(BWOH-nah SEH-rah)

Howdy
Come va?
(KOH-meh vah)

Greetings
Saluti
(sah-LOO-tee)

Salutations
Saluti
(sah-LOO-tee)

What's up?
Cosa c'è di nuovo?
(KOH-sah cheh dee NOO-voh)

How are you?
Come stai?
(KOH-meh STAH-ee)

How's it going?
Come va?
(KOH-meh vah)

Howdy-do
Come va?
(KOH-meh vah)

Hiya
Ciao
(chow)

Yo
Ehi
(EH-ee)

Long time no see
Siamo passati tanto tempo
(see-AH-moh pahs-SAH-tee TAHN-toh TEM-poh)

Nice to see you
Piacere di vederti
(pyah-CHEH-reh dee veh-DEHR-tee)

Pleasure to meet you
Piacere di conoscerti
(pyah-CHEH-reh dee koh-noh-SHEHR-tee)

It's been a while
È passato un po' di tempo
(eh pahs-SAH-toh oon poh dee TEM-poh)

What's new?
Cosa c'è di nuovo?
(KOH-sah cheh dee NOO-voh)

How have you been?
Come stai?
(KOH-meh STAH-ee)

How's everything?
Come va tutto?
(KOH-meh vah TOOT-toh)

What's happening?
Che succede?
(keh soo-CHEH-deh)

How are things?
Come va tutto?
(KOH-meh vah TOOT-toh)

Hey there
Ciao
(chow)

Morning
Buongiorno
(BWOHN-jor-noh)

Afternoon
Buon pomeriggio
(BWOHN poh-meh-REE-joh)

Evening
Buona sera
(BWOH-nah SEH-rah)

Good to see you
È bello vederti
(eh BEHL-loh veh-DEHR-tee)

Welcome
Benvenuto
(BEHN-veh-noo-toh)

Cheers
Salute
(sah-LOO-teh)

Hola
Ciao
(chow)

Bonjour
Buongiorno
(BWOHN-jor-noh)

Konnichiwa
Konnichiwa
(kohn-nee-CHEE-wah)

Ciao
Ciao
(chow)

Namaste
Namaste
(nah-MAH-steh)

Shalom
Shalom
(shah-LOHM)

Salaam
Salam
(sah-LAHM)

Zdravstvuyte
Zdravstvuyte
(zdrah-stvoo-YEH-tyeh)

Ahlan
Ciao
(chow)

BANKING

I need to make a deposit.
Ho bisogno di fare un de-posi-to.
(oh BEE-zoh-nyoh dee FAH-reh oon deh-POH-si-toh)

I want to withdraw some cash.
Vorrei prelevare del denaro.
(vohr-RAY preh-leh-VAH-reh del deh-NAH-roh)

Can I open a new account?
Posso aprire un nuovo conto?
(POHs-soh ah-PREE-reh oon NU-o-vo KOHN-toh)

I need to update my account information.
Devo aggiornare le informazioni del mio conto.
(DEH-vo ah-JOR-nah-reh leh in-for-ma-TZYO-nee del MEE-oh KOHN-toh)

I want to apply for a loan.
Vorrei richiedere un prestito.
(vohr-RAY ree-kyeh-DEH-reh oon preh-STEE-toh)

Can you help me with a wire transfer?
Puoi aiutarmi con un trasferimento bancario?
(POO-oy ah-yoo-TAHR-mee kon oon TRAS-feh-ree-MEN-toh ban-KA-ryo)

I need to cash a check.
Devo incassare un assegno.
(DEH-vo een-kah-SAH-reh oon as-SEH-nyoh)

Can I get some change, please?
Potrei avere del resto, per favore?
(po-TREH-ee ah-VEH-reh del REH-stoh, pehr fa-VOH-reh)

I need to pay some bills.
Devo pagare delle bollette.
(DEH-vo pah-GAH-reh DEL-leh boh-LET-teh)

I want to order some checks.
Vorrei ordinare degli assegno.
(vohr-RAY or-dee-NA-reh DEH-jee ah-SEH-nyee)

I want to set up direct deposit.
Vorrei impostare il deposito diretto.
(vohr-RAY im-PO-stah-reh eel deh-POH-si-toh dee-REH-ttoh)

Can I get a copy of my statement?
Posso avere una copia del mio estratto conto?
(POHs-soh ah-VEH-reh OO-nah KOH-pyah del MEE-oh es-TRAH-toh KOHN-toh)

I need to dispute a charge.
Devo contestare una spesa.
(DEH-vo kon-teh-STAH-reh OO-nah SPEH-sah)

Can I get a cashier's check?
Posso avere un assegno circolare?
(POHs-soh ah-VEH-reh oon as-SEH-nyoh cheer-ko-LAH-reh)

I want to close my account.
Voglio chiudere il mio conto.
(VO-lyoh kyoo-DEH-reh eel MEE-oh KOHN-toh)

Can you help me activate my debit card?
Puoi aiutarmi ad attivare la mia carta di debito?
(POO-oy ah-yoo-TAHR-mee ad aht-tee-VAH-reh lah MEE-ah KAHR-tah dee deh-BEE-toh)

I want to know my account balance.
Vorrei sapere il saldo del mio conto.
(vohr-RAY sah-PEH-reh eel SAHL-doh del MEE-oh KOHN-toh)

Can I get a loan application form?
Posso avere un modulo di richiesta di prestito?
(POHs-soh ah-VEH-reh oon MO-doo-loh dee ree-kyeh-stah dee preh-STEE-toh)

I need to transfer money to another account.
Devo trasferire denaro su un altro conto.
(DEH-vo trahs-feh-REE-reh deh-NAH-roh soo oon AL-troh KOHN-toh)

Can I speak to a bank representative?
Posso parlare con un rappresentante della banca?
(POHs-soh par-LAH-reh kon oon rap-preh-sen-TAHN-teh deh-lah BAHN-kah)

I want to change my account type.
Vorrei cambiare il tipo di mio conto.
(vohr-RAY kahm-BYA-reh eel TEE-po dee MEE-oh KOHN-toh)

Can you help me order a new debit card?
Puoi aiutarmi ad ordinare una nuova carta di debito?
(POO-oy ah-yoo-TAHR-mee ad or-dee-NAH-reh OO-nah NOO-oh-vah KAHR-tah dee deh-BEE-toh)

I need to update my contact information.
Devo aggiornare le mie informazioni di contatto.
(DEH-vo ah-JOR-nah-reh leh MEE-eh in-for-ma-TZYO-nee dee kon-TAH-toh)

Can I get a safe deposit box?
Posso avere una cassaforte?
(POHs-soh ah-VEH-reh OO-nah kas-sah-FOR-teh)

I want to know my account number.
Vorrei sapere il mio numero di conto.
(vohr-RAY sah-PEH-reh eel MEE-oh NOO-meh-roh dee KOHN-toh)

Can I get a bank statement?
Posso avere un estratto conto?
(POHs-soh ah-VEH-reh oon es-TRAH-toh KOHN-toh)

I need to update my beneficiary information.
Devo aggiornare le informazioni del mio beneficiario.
(DEH-vo ah-JOR-nah-reh leh in-for-ma-TZYO-nee del MEE-oh beh-neh-fee-tsyah-REE-oh)

I want to dispute a transaction.
Voglio contestare una transazione.
(VOHL-yoh kohn-tes-TAH-reh OO-nah trahn-sah-TSYOH-neh)

Can I get a cashier's check?
Posso avere un assegno circolare?
(POHs-soh ah-VEH-reh oon ah-SAY-nyoh cheer-koh-LAH-reh)

I need to close my account.
Devo chiudere il mio conto.
(DEH-vo kee-YOO-deh-reh eel MEE-oh KOHN-toh)

Can you help me set up online banking?
Puoi aiutarmi ad attivare la banca online?
(POO-oy ah-yoo-TAHR-mee ad aht-tee-VAH-reh lah BAHN-kah on-LINE)

I want to open a savings account.
Vorrei aprire un conto di risparmio RISPARMIO.
(vohr-RAY ah-PREE-reh oon KOHN-toh dee ree-SPAR-mee-oh)

Can I deposit a check?
Posso depositare un assegno?
(POHs-soh deh-poh-zee-TAH-reh oon ah-SAY-nyoh)

I need to withdraw cash.
Devo prelevare del contante.
(DEH-vo preh-leh-VAH-reh del kohn-TAHN-teh)

Can I get a money order?
Posso avere un vaglia postale?
(POHs-soh ah-VEH-reh oon VAHL-yah poh-STAH-leh)

I want to know my routing number.
Vorrei sapere il mio codice ABI.
(vohr-RAY sah-PEH-reh eel MEE-oh KOH-dee-cheh AH-bee)

Can I get a foreign currency exchange?
Posso cambiare valuta estera?
(POHs-soh kahm-BYA-reh vah-LOO-tah eh-STE-rah)

I need to update my personal information.
Devo aggiornare le mie informazioni personali.
(DEH-vo ah-JOR-nah-reh leh MEE-eh in-for-ma-TZYO-nee per-soh-NAH-lee)

Can you help me enroll in mobile banking?
Puoi aiutarmi ad iscrivermi alla banca mobile?
(POO-oy ah-yoo-TAHR-mee ad ees-kree-VEHR-mee AH-lah BAHN-kah moh-BEE-leh)

Is there a fee for using an ATM?
C'è una tassa per l'uso di un bancomat?
(CHEH oo-nah TAH-sah pehr LOO-soh dee oon BAHN-koh-maht?)

COMMON TRAVELER QUESTIONS

What is the local currency and exchange rate?
Qual è la valuta locale e il tasso di cambio?
(KWAHL eh lah vah-LOO-tah LOH-kah-leh eh eel TAHS-soh dee KAHM-bee-oh)

What are the best modes of transportation in the area?
Quali sono i migliori modi di trasporto in zona?
(KWAH-lee SOH-noh ee MEE-glyoh-ree MOH-dee dee trah-SPOR-toh een ZOH-nah)

What is the best time of year to visit?
Qual è il momento migliore dell'anno per visitare?
(KWAH-lee eel moh-MEN-toh MEE-glyoh-reh dell-YAH-noh pehr vee-zee-TAH-reh)

What are the must-see tourist attractions?
Quali sono le attrazioni turistiche da non perdere?
(KWAH-lee SOH-noh leh aht-trah-TSEE-oh-nee too-ree-STEE-keh dah non PEHR-deh-reh)

What are the local customs and traditions?
Quali sono le usanze e le tradizioni locali?
(KWAH-lee SOH-noh leh oo-ZAHN-tseh eh leh trah-dee-TSYOH-nee LOH-kah-lee)

How do I get around using public transportation?
Come ci si sposta con i mezzi pubblici?
(KOH-meh chee see SPHOH-stah kohn ee MEH-tsee POO-blee-chee)

What are the most popular local foods?
Quali sono i cibi locali più popolari?
(KWAH-lee SOH-noh ee CHEE-bee LOH-kah-lee p'yoo poh-POH-lah-ree)

What vaccinations are required for travel to this destination?
Quali vaccinazioni sono richieste per viaggiare in questa destinazione?
*(KWAH-lee vahk-tsee-nah-TSYOH-nee SOH-noh ree-KWEE-eh-steh pehr
vee-ah-JYAH-reh een KWEH-stah deh-stee-NAH-tsyoh-neh)*

What is the local weather like?
Che tempo fa in zona?
(keh TEHM-poh fah een ZOH-nah)

How much should I budget for my trip?
Quanto dovrei budgettare per il mio viaggio?
*(KWAHN-toh DOH-vreh-ee BOO-jet-TAH-reh pehr eel MEE-oh
vee-AH-djoh)*

What is the best way to book accommodation?
Qual è il modo migliore per prenotare l'alloggio?
*(KWAH-lee eel MOH-doh MEE-glyoh-reh pehr preh-noh-TAH-reh
lah-LOH-djoh)*

What is the local language and do people speak English?
Qual è la lingua locale e la gente parla inglese?
*(KWAH-lee eh lah LEEN-gwah LOH-kah-leh eh lah JEN-teh PAHR-lah
een-GLEH-zeh)*

What is the best way to get from the airport to my accommodation?
Qual è il modo migliore per arrivare dall'aeroporto al mio alloggio?
*(KWAH-lee eel MOH-doh MEE-glyoh-reh pehr ah-REE-vah-reh
dahl-LAH-eh-roh-POHR-toh ahl MEE-oh ah-LOH-djoh)*

Are there any local festivals or events happening during my visit?
Ci sono feste o eventi locali durante il mio soggiorno?
*(chee SOH-noh FEHS-teh oh eh-VEHN-tee LOH-kah-lee doo-RAN-teh eel
MEE-oh soh-JOHHR-noh)*

What is the tipping culture like in this area?
Come funziona la cultura del lasciare la mancia in questa zona?
*(KOH-meh foon-tsee-OH-nah lah KOOl-too-rah del lah-SHAH-ree lah
MAHN-chee-ah een KWEH-stah ZOH-nah)*

Are there any local markets or shopping areas worth visiting?
Ci sono mercati o zone commerciali locali che valgono la pena visitare?
(chee SOH-noh MEHR-kah-tee oh ZOH-neh koh-mehr-chee-AH-lee
LOH-kah-lee keh VAHL-goh-noh lah PEH-nah vee-zee-TAH-reh)

How do I navigate the public transportation system?
Come navigare il sistema di trasporto pubblico?
(KOH-meh nah-vee-GAH-reh eel SY-steh-mah dee trah-SPOR-toh
POO-blee-coh)

What are the emergency numbers in this area?
Quali sono i numeri di emergenza in questa zona?
(KWAH-lee SOH-noh ee NOO-meh-ree dee eh-mehr-DJEN-tsa een
KWEH-stah ZONA?)

Can you recommend any good restaurants or cafes?
Puoi consigliarmi dei buoni ristoranti o caffè?
(PWOH-ee kohn-see-LYAR-mee deh-ee BWOH-nee rees-toh-RAHN-tee
oh KAH-feh)

Is the tap water safe to drink here?
L'acqua del rubinetto è potabile qui?
(LAH-kwah dehl roo-bee-NET-toh eh poh-TAH-bee-leh kwee)

How do I access the internet while traveling here?
Come posso accedere a Internet durante il mio viaggio qui?
(KOH-meh POHs-soh ah-CHES-seh-deh ah een-ter-NET doo-RAN-teh eel
MEE-oh vyah-joh kwee)

What are some popular local dishes or foods I should try?
Quali sono alcuni piatti o cibi locali popolari che dovrei provare?
(KWAH-lee SOH-noh ahl-KOO-nee PEE-ah-tee oh CHEE-bee LOH-kah-lee
poh-poh-LAH-ree keh DOH-vreh-ee proh-VAH-reh)

How do I make local phone calls from my cell phone?
Come faccio a fare chiamate locali dal mio cellulare?
(KOH-meh FAH-chyoh ah FAH-reh KYAH-mah-teh LOH-kah-lee dahl
MEE-oh chehl-luh-LAH-reh)

What are the must-see tourist attractions in this area?
Quali sono le attrazioni turistiche da non perdere in questa zona?
(KWAH-lee SOH-noh leh ah-trah-TSYOH-nee too-ree-STEE-keh dah non pehr-DEH-reh een KWEH-stah ZOH-nah)

Are there any local tours or excursions I can book?
Ci sono tour o escursioni locali che posso prenotare?
(chee SOH-noh toor oh eh-skoor-SYOH-nee LOH-kah-lee keh POHs-soh preh-noh-TAH-reh)

What is the best way to exchange currency here?
Qual è il modo migliore per cambiare valuta qui?
(KWAH-lee eel MOH-doh MEE-glyoh-reh pehr kahm-BYAH-reh vah-LOO-tah kwee)

Are credit cards widely accepted in this area?
Le carte di credito sono ampiamente accettate in questa zona?
(leh KAHR-teh dee KREH-dee-toh SOH-noh ahm-pee-AHM-teh ah-ches-SEH-teh een KWEH-stah ZOH-nah)

Can you recommend any good day trips from here?
Puoi consigliarmi delle belle gite di un giorno da qui?
(PWOH-ee kohn-see-LYAR-mee DEH-leh BEHL-leh JEE-teh dee oon JOHR-noh dah kwee)

Is it safe to walk around at night in this area?
È sicuro camminare di notte in questa zona?
(eh see-KOO-roh kahm-mee-NAH-reh dee NOHT-teh een KWEH-stah ZOH-nah)

How do I get to the nearest pharmacy?
Come posso arrivare alla farmacia più vicina?
(KOH-meh POHs-soh ah-ree-VAH-reh AHL-lah far-MAH-chyah PEE-oo vee-CHEE-nah)

Are there any local customs or traditions I should be aware of?
Ci sono usanze o tradizioni locali di cui dovrei essere a conoscenza?
(chee SOH-noh oo-ZAHN-tseh oh trah-dee-TSYOH-nee LOH-kah-lee dee kwee DOH-vreh-ee EHs-seh-reh ah koh-NOS-chen-tsyah)

What is the best way to get around the city/town?
Qual è il modo migliore per spostarsi in città/paese?
(KWAH-lee eel MOH-doh MEE-glyoh-reh pehr spoh-STAH-see een
CHEET-tah/PAH-eh-zeh)

How do I purchase tickets for public transportation?
Come posso acquistare i biglietti per i trasporti pubblici?
(KOH-meh POHs-soh ah-kwee-STAH-reh ee beel-LYET-tee pehr ee
trah-SPOHR-tee POOB-blee-chee)

Can you recommend any good shopping areas or markets?
Puoi consigliarmi delle buone zone commerciali o mercati?
(PWOH-ee kohn-see-LYAR-mee DEH-leh BWOH-neh ZOH-neh
koh-mehr-CHYAH-lee oh mehr-KAH-tee)

How do I ask for help if I have an emergency?
Come chiedo aiuto in caso di emergenza?
(KOH-meh KYEH-doh ah-YOO-toh een KA-zoh dee eh-MEHR-jehn-tsah)

What is the best way to get from the airport to my hotel?
Qual è il modo migliore per raggiungere l'hotel dall'aeroporto?
(KWAH-lee eel MOH-doh MEE-glyoh-reh pehr rah-JOO-neh-reh
LOH-tehl dahl-lah-eh-roh-POHR-toh)

COMMON RESPONSES TO QUESTIONS

Yes, that's correct.
Sì, è corretto.
(SEE, eh koh-REHT-toh)

No, that's not quite right.
No, non è proprio corretto.
(NOH, non eh PROH-pree-oh koh-REHT-toh)

I'm not sure, let me check.
Non sono sicuro/a, lasciami controllare.
(non SOH-noh see-KOO-roh/ah, lah-SHA-mee kon-troh-LAH-reh)

I don't know, sorry.
Non lo so, mi dispiace.
(non loh soh, mee dee-SPYA-cheh)

Can you repeat the question, please?
Puoi ripetere la domanda, per favore?
(pwoh-ee ree-peh-TEH-reh lah doh-MAHN-dah, pehr fah-VOH-reh?)

I'm sorry, I didn't catch that.
Mi dispiace, non ho capito.
(mee dee-SPYA-cheh, non oh kah-PEE-toh)

Absolutely!
Assolutamente!
(ah-soh-loo-ta-MEN-teh!)

Definitely not.
Decisamente no.
(deh-chee-za-MEN-teh noh)

Maybe, I need more information to give a proper answer.
Forse, ho bisogno di più informazioni per darti una risposta adeguata.
(FOR-seh, oh bee-SOH-nyoh dee p'yoo in-for-ma-TSYOH-nee pehr DAR-tee OO-nah ree-SPHO-sta ah-deh-GWA-tah)

It depends.
Dipende.
(dee-PEN-deh)

That's a good question.
È una buona domanda.
(eh OO-nah BOO-nah doh-MAHN-dah)

I'm afraid I can't help you with that.
Mi spiace, non posso aiutarti con questo.
(mee SPYA-cheh, non POH-soh ah-yoo-TAHR-tee kon KWEH-stoh)

I'm sorry, I can't disclose that information.
Mi dispiace, non posso divulgare queste informazioni.
(mee dee-SPYA-cheh, non POH-soh dee-vool-GAH-reh KWEH-steh in-for-ma-TSYOH-nee)

Yes, of course.
Sì, certo.
(SEE, CHEHR-toh)

No, I don't think so.
No, non credo.
(NOH, non KREH-doh)

I'm sorry, I can't do that.
Mi dispiace, non posso farlo.
(mee dee-SPYA-cheh, non POH-soh FAHR-loh)

That's up to you.
Dipende da te.
(dee-PEN-deh dah teh)

Let me think about it for a moment.
Fammi pensare per un momento.
(FAHM-mee pehn-SAH-reh pehr oon moh-MEN-toh)

Sorry, I'm not familiar with that.
Mi dispiace, non sono familiare con quello.
(mee dee-SPYA-cheh, non SOH-noh fa-mee-lyah-reh kon KWEH-loh)

That's a great idea!
È un'ottima idea!
(eh oon-ot-TEE-mah EE-deh-ah!)

I'm sorry, I didn't mean to offend you.
Mi dispiace, non volevo offenderti.
(mee dee-SPYA-cheh, non voh-LEH-voh oh-fen-DEHR-tee)

That's possible, but I'm not certain.
È possibile, ma non sono certo/a.
(eh pos-SEE-beh-leh, ma non SOH-noh cher-toh/ah)

That's not my area of expertise.
Questo non è la mia area di competenza.
(KWEH-stoh non eh lah MEE-ah AH-reh-ah dee kohm-peh-TSEN-tsa)

Sorry, I don't have that information at the moment.
Scusa, al momento non ho queste informazioni.
(SKOO-sah, al moh-MEN-toh non oh KWEH-steh in-for-ma-TSYOH-nee)

That sounds interesting!
Sembra interessante!
(SEM-bra een-teh-REH-san-teh!)

I'm not sure, let me get back to you on that.
Non sono sicuro/a, ti farò sapere.
(non SOH-noh see-KOO-roh/ah, tee fah-ROH sah-PEH-reh)

That's not my decision to make.
Non spetta a me decidere.
(non SPEH-tah ah meh deh-chee-DEH-reh)

Sorry, I don't have an answer for you.
Scusa, non ho una risposta per te.
(SKOO-sah, non oh oo-nah ree-SPHO-stah pehr teh)

That's a good point.
Hai ragione.
(hai rah-JOH-neh)

I'm not sure, I'll have to look into it.
Non sono sicuro/a, dovrò approfondire la questione.
(non SOH-noh see-KOO-roh/ah, doh-VROH ap-pro-fon-DEE-reh lah kweh-STYO-neh)

I'm sorry, I can't do that for you.
Mi dispiace, non posso farlo per te.
(mee dee-SPYA-cheh, non POH-soh FAHR-loh pehr teh)

I see what you mean.
Capisco quello che intendi.
(ka-PEES-koh KWEH-loh keh een-TEN-dee)

Sorry, I don't have time for that right now.
Scusa, non ho tempo per questo adesso.
(SKOO-sah, non oh TEM-po pehr KWEH-stoh ah-DESS-soh)

That's a valid point.
È un punto valido.
(eh oon PON-toh vah-LEE-doh)

Let me think about it and get back to you.
Fammi pensarci e ti faccio sapere.
(FAH-mee pen-SAHR-chee eh tee FAH-choh sah-PEH-reh)

That's a good question.
È una buona domanda.
(eh OO-nah BWOH-nah doh-MAN-dah)

I'm not quite sure what you mean.

Non sono del tutto sicuro/a di capire cosa intendi.

(non SOH-noh del TOHL-toh see-KOO-roh/ah dee kah-PEE-reh KOH-sah een-TEN-dee)

I'm sorry, I don't know how to help you with that.

Mi dispiace, non so come aiutarti con questo.

(mee dee-SPYA-cheh, non soh KOH-meh ah-yoo-TAHR-tee kon KWEH-stoh)

I think so, but let me confirm and get back to you.

Penso di sì, ma lasciami confermare e ti faccio sapere.

(PEN-soh dee see, ma lah-SHAH-mee kon-fer-MAH-reh eh tee FAH-choh sah-PEH-reh)

I'm sorry, but I don't have the authority to do that.

Mi dispiace, ma non ho l'autorità per farlo.

(mee dee-SPYA-cheh, ma non oh lah-oo-toh-REE-tah pehr FAHR-loh)

PETS

Dogs
Cani
(KA-nee)

Cats
Gatti
(GA-ti)

Fish
Pesci
(PEH-shee)

Birds
Uccelli
(oo-CHEL-lee)

Hamsters
Criceti
(kri-CHEH-tee)

Guinea pigs
Cavie
(KAH-vee-eh)

Rabbits
Conigli
(co-NEE-lyi)

Ferrets
Furetti
(foo-REH-tee)

Turtles
Tartarughe
(tar-ta-ROO-geh)

Lizards
Lucertole
(loo-cher-TOH-leh)

Snakes
Serpenti
(ser-PEN-tee)

Tarantulas
Tarantole
(tah-rahn-TOH-leh)

Hermit crabs
Granchi eremita
(gran-kee eh-reh-MEE-ta)

Hedgehogs
Ricci
(REE-chee)

Chinchillas
Cincillà
(chin-CHIL-la)

Gerbils
Gerbilli
(jer-BIL-lee)

Rats
Ratti
(RAH-tee)

Mice
Topi
(TOH-pee)

Sugar gliders
Petauri dello zucchero
(peh-TOW-ree DEHL-loh zoo-KER-ro)

Axolotls
Axolotl
(ahk-soh-LOH-tl)

Bearded dragons
Drachi barbuti
(DRAH-kee bar-BOO-tee)

Iguanas
Iguane
(ee-GWAH-neh)

Tortoises
Tartarughe terrestri
(tar-ta-ROO-geh ter-RES-tree)

Miniature horses
Cavalli in miniatura
(ka-VAL-lee een mee-nee-AH-too-rah)

Ferrets
Furetti
(foo-REH-tee)

Snails
Lumache
(loo-MAH-keh)

Frogs
Rane
(RAH-neh)

Crayfish
Gamberetti d'acqua dolce
(gam-beh-REH-tee dah-kwah DOHLcheh)

Shrimp
Gamberi
(gam-BEH-ree)

Cichlids
Ciclidi
(chee-KLEE-dee)

Guppies
Guppy
(GUHP-pee)

COLORS

Red
Rosso
(ROSS-o)

Orange
Arancione
(ah-ran-CHYO-neh)

Yellow
Giallo
(JAL-lo)

Green
Verde
(VER-deh)

Blue
Blu
(BLOO)

Purple
Viola
(VEE-oh-lah)

Pink
Rosa
(ROH-zah)

Brown
Marrone
(mar-ROH-neh)

Gray
Grigio
(GREE-joh)

White
Bianco
(BYAHN-koh)

Black
Nero
(NEH-roh)

Magenta
Magenta
(mah-JEN-tah)

Lavender
Lavanda
(lah-VAN-dah)

Indigo
Indaco
(een-DAH-koh)

Turquoise
Turchese
(TOOR-keh-zeh)

Gold
Oro
(OH-roh)

Silver
Argento
(ahr-JEN-toh)

Beige
Beige
(BAY-zheh)

Cream
Crema
(KREH-mah)

Maroon
Bordeaux
(bor-DOH)

Teal
Turchese
(TOOR-keh-zeh)

Coral
Corallo
(ko-RAHL-lo)

Navy
Blu scuro
(BLOO SKOO-roh)

Olive
Oliva
(oh-LEE-vah)

Peach
Pesca
(PEH-skah)

Fuchsia
Fucsia
(FOOK-syah)

Sky Blue
Azzurro
(aht-SOOR-roh)

Burgundy
Borgogna
(bor-GO-nyah)

Forest Green
Verde bosco
(VER-deh BOHS-koh)

Salmon
Salmone
(sal-MOH-neh)

Rust
Ruggine
(roo-JEE-neh)

Tan
Marrone chiaro
(mar-ROH-neh key-AH-roh)

Lilac
Lilla
(LEE-lah)

Mustard
Senape
(seh-NAH-peh)

Periwinkle
Celeste
(cheh-LES-teh)

NUMBERS

One
Uno
(OO-noh)

Two
Due
(DOO-eh)

Three
Tre
(TREH)

Four
Quattro
(KWAH-troh)

Five
Cinque
(CHEEN-kweh)

Six
Sei
(SEH-ee)

Seven
Sette
(SEH-teh)

Eight
Otto
(OHT-toh)

Nine
Nove
(NOH-veh)

Ten
Dieci
(DYEH-chee)

HANDLING A RUDE PERSON

I understand you're upset, but please don't take it out on me.
Io capisco che sei arrabbiato, ma per favore non prendertela con me.
*(EE-o kah-PEES-koh keh say ah-rah-BYA-toh, mah pehr fah-VOH-reh
non PREHN-dehr-teh-lah kohn meh)*

**I'm sorry you feel that way, but I will not tolerate being spoken to in
that manner.**
Mi dispiace che ti senti così, ma non tollererò di essere parlato in quel
modo.
*(Mee dee-SPYA-cheh keh tee SEN-tee KAW-tzee, mah non
TOHL-leh-reh-roh dee eh-SEH-reh par-LAH-toh een kwel MOH-doh)*

Let's try to keep this conversation civil.
Cerchiamo di mantenere questa conversazione civile.
*(Chehr-kee-AH-moh dee mahn-teh-NEH-reh KWEHS-tah
kon-ver-sa-TSYOH-neh CHEE-vee-leh)*

I'm happy to help you, but please speak to me with respect.
Sono felice di aiutarti, ma per favore parla con me con rispetto.
*(SOH-noh FEH-lee-cheh dee ah-yoo-TAR-tee, mah pehr fah-VOH-reh
PAHR-lah kohn meh kohn ree-SPET-toh)*

I hear what you're saying, but there's no need to be rude.
Capisco quello che dici, ma non c'è bisogno di essere maleducato.
*(Kah-PEES-koh KWEL-loh keh DEE-chee, mah non cheh bee-ZOHN-doh
dee eh-SEH-reh mah-leh-doo-KAH-toh)*

I don't appreciate the tone you're using with me.
Non apprezzo il tono che usi con me.
(Non ah-PRET-tsoh eel TOH-noh keh OO-see kohn meh)

Let's take a break and come back to this conversation when we can be more respectful to each other.
Facciamo una pausa e riprendiamo questa conversazione quando possiamo essere più rispettosi l'uno con l'altro.
(FAH-chya-moh OO-nah POW-zah eh ree-PREN-dee-ah-moh KWEHS-tah kon-ver-sa-TSYOH-neh KWAHN-do POSS-ya-moh EH-seh-reh pew ree-speh-TOH-see LOO-noh kohn lAHL-troh)

I'm sorry you're having a bad day, but that doesn't give you the right to be rude to me.
Mi dispiace che tu abbia una brutta giornata, ma questo non ti dà il diritto di essere maleducato con me.
(Mee dee-SPYA-cheh keh too AHB-bee-ah OO-nah BROO-tah jor-NAH-tah, mah KWES-toh non tee dah eel DEER-ree-toh dee EH-seh-reh mah-leh-doo-KAH-toh kohn meh)

I'm willing to listen to your concerns, but please express them in a respectful manner.
Sono disposto ad ascoltare le tue preoccupazioni, ma per favore esprimile in modo rispettoso.
(SOH-noh dee-SPAW-stoh ahd ah-SKOHL-tah-reh leh TOO-eh preh-ohk-koo-PATSYOH-nee, mah pehr fah-VOH-reh ehs-PREE-mee-leh een MOH-doh rees-peh-TOH-soh)

I don't appreciate being spoken to in that manner.
Non tollero di essere parlato in quel modo.
(Non tohl-LEH-roh dee eh-SEH-reh par-LAH-toh een kwel MOH-doh)

I understand that you're frustrated, but that's not an excuse to be rude to me.
Capisco che sei frustrato, ma non è un'escusa per essere maleducato con me.
(Kah-PEES-koh keh say froo-STRAH-toh, mah non eh oon-eh-SKOO-sah pehr EH-seh-reh mah-leh-doo-KAH-toh kohn meh)

I'm happy to help you, but I won't tolerate being treated disrespectfully.
Sono felice di aiutarti, ma non tollero di essere trattato con mancanza di rispetto.
(SOH-noh FEH-lee-cheh dee ah-yoo-TAR-tee, mah non tohl-LEH-roh dee eh-SEH-reh trah-TAH-toh kohn MAHN-kahn-tsah dee rees-PEHT-toh)

I don't appreciate your tone.
Non apprezzo il tuo tono.
(Non ah-PRET-tsoh eel TOO-oh too-oh-oh)

Let's stay focused on finding a solution, rather than arguing with each other.
Rimaniamo concentrati nell'individuare una soluzione, anziché litigare l'uno con l'altro.
(Ree-mah-NYA-moh KOHN-tsehn-TRAH-tee nehl-een-dee-VAH-reh OO-nah soh-loo-TSYOH-neh, ahn-TSEE-keh lee-TEE-gah-reh LOO-noh kohn lAHL-troh)

I'm sorry, but I won't tolerate being spoken to in that manner.
Mi dispiace, ma non tollererò di essere parlato in quel modo.
(Mee dee-SPYA-cheh, mah non tohl-leh-REH-roh dee eh-SEH-reh par-LAH-toh een kwel MOH-doh)

Let's take a break and come back to this conversation when we're both feeling more calm.
Facciamo una pausa e riprendiamo questa conversazione quando siamo entrambi più calmi.
(FAH-chya-moh OO-nah POW-zah eh ree-PREN-dee-ah-moh KWEHS-tah kon-ver-sa-TSYOH-neh KWAN-doh SYAH-moh en-TROHM-bee p-yoo KAHL-mee)

I won't be spoken to in that manner, so please change your tone.
Non voglio essere parlato in quel modo, per favore cambia tono.
(Non VOH-lyoh eh-SEH-reh par-LAH-toh een kwel MOH-doh, pehr fah-VOH-reh KAHM-byah TOH-noh)

I don't appreciate your attitude.
Non apprezzo il tuo atteggiamento.
(Non ah-PRET-tsoh eel TOO-oh ah-tayd-jah-MEN-toh)

Let's try to understand each other's perspectives and find a solution together.
Cerchiamo di comprendere le prospettive reciproche e trovare insieme una soluzione.
(Chehr-KEE-ah-moh dee kohm-PREN-deh-reh leh proh-speh-TY-veh reh-kree-OH-keh eh troh-VAH-reh een-SEE-meh oon-ah soh-loo-TSYOH-neh)

I won't engage in this conversation if you continue to be disrespectful.
Non parteciperò a questa conversazione se continui a mancare di rispetto.
(Non pahr-teh-chee-peh-ROh ah KWEHS-tah kon-ver-sa-TSYOH-neh seh kohn-TEE-noo-ee ah MAHN-kah-reh dee rees-PEHT-toh)

Please don't speak to me like that.
Per favore, non parlarmi così.
(Pehr fah-VOH-reh, non par-LAHR-mee KOH-zee)

I'm happy to discuss this with you, but we need to maintain a respectful tone.
Sono felice di discutere questo con te, ma dobbiamo mantenere un tono rispettoso.
(SOH-noh FEH-lee-cheh dee dee-SKOO-teh-reh KWE-stoh kohn teh, mah dohb-BYAH-moh mahn-TEH-neh-reh oon TOH-noh rees-peh-TOH-soh)

Let's try to find a compromise that works for both of us.
Cerchiamo di trovare un compromesso che funzioni per entrambi.
(Chehr-KEE-ah-moh dee troh-VAH-reh oon kom-PROM-ehs-soh keh FOON-tsyoh-nee pehr en-TRAHM-bee)

Your behavior is unacceptable.
Il tuo comportamento non è accettabile.
(Eel TOO-oh kohm-PORT-men-toh non eh aht-cheh-TAH-beh-leh)

I understand that you may be upset, but that doesn't give you the right to speak to me that way.
Capisco che potresti essere arrabbiato, ma questo non ti dà il diritto di parlarmi in quel modo.
(KAH-pee-skoh keh poh-TREH-stee eh-SEH-reh ah-rahb-BYA-toh, mah KWES-toh non tee dah eel deer-RYE-toh dee par-LAR-mee een kwel MOH-doh)

Let's try to focus on finding a solution instead of getting caught up in arguing.
Cerchiamo di concentrarci sulla ricerca di una soluzione invece di rimanere bloccati in una discussione.
(Chehr-KEE-ah-moh dee kohn-tsen-TRAHR-chee SOO-lah ree-KER-kah dee REE-kay-brah-tsee een-VEH-cheh dee ree-SPON-see-OH-neh)

Please speak to me in a more polite manner.
Per favore, parlami in modo più educato.
(Pehr fah-VOH-reh, par-LAH-mee een MOH-doh p-yoo eh-doo-KAH-toh)

I don't appreciate being spoken to in that tone.
Non apprezzo di essere parlato in quel tono.
(Non ah-PRET-tsoh dee eh-SEH-reh par-LAH-toh een kwel TOH-noh)

Let's try to approach this conversation with an open mind and willingness to listen.
Cerchiamo di affrontare questa conversazione con una mente aperta e la volontà di ascoltare.
(Chehr-KEE-ah-moh dee ahff-ron-TAH-reh KWE-stah kon-ver-sa-TSYOH-neh kohn OO-nah MEEN-teh ah-PEHR-tah eh lah voh-LOHN-tee dee ah-SKOHL-tah-reh)

Please don't interrupt me while I'm speaking.
Per favore, non interrompermi mentre sto parlando.
(Pehr fah-VOH-reh, non een-teh-rohm-PEHR-mee men-treh sto pahr-LAHN-doh)

I refuse to be treated this way, so I'm ending this conversation now.
Rifiuto di essere trattato in questo modo, quindi sto terminando
questa conversazione adesso.
(Ree-foo-toh dee eh-SEH-reh trah-TAH-toh een KWE-stoh MOH-doh,
kwen-DEE STOH teh-ree-mee-NAHN-doh KWE-stah
kon-ver-sa-TSYOH-neh ah-DEHS-soh)

Let's try to find common ground and work towards a resolution.
Cerchiamo di trovare un terreno comune e lavorare verso una
soluzione.
(Chehr-KEE-ah-moh dee troh-VAH-reh oon teh-REH-noh koh-MOO-neh
eh la-VOH-ree-ah-reh VEHR-soh oon-ah soo-LU-tsyoh-neh)

I will not tolerate being treated this way any longer.
Non tollererò di essere trattato in questo modo per ancora molto
tempo.
(Non tohl-leh-reh-ROH dee eh-SEH-reh trah-TAH-toh een KWE-stoh
MOH-doh pehr ahn-KOH-rah MOHL-toh TEM-poh)

**Let's take a break and come back to this conversation later when we
can both be calmer.**
Prendiamo una pausa e torniamo a questa conversazione più tardi
quando possiamo essere entrambi più calmi.
(Pren-DEE-ah-moh OOH-nah POW-zah eh tor-NYA-moh ah KWE-stah
kon-ver-sa-TSYOH-neh pyoo TAR-dee kwan-do POHS-see-ah-moh
EHn-trahm-bee pyoo KAHL-mee)

Your words are hurtful and unnecessary.
Le tue parole sono offese e non necessarie.
(Leh TOO-eh pah-ROH-leh SOH-noh ohf-FEH-zeh eh non
ne-ches-SAH-ree-eh)

**I don't believe this conversation is productive, so I think we should
end it now.**
Non credo che questa conversazione sia produttiva, quindi penso che
dovremmo finirla adesso.
(Non KREH-doh keh KWE-stah kon-ver-sa-TSYOH-neh see-ah
pro-DUT-tee-vah, KWEHN-dee pehn-soh keh dohv-REHM-moh
FIN-ee-lah ah-DEHs-soh)

I deserve to be treated with respect and dignity, just like you do.

Merezzo di essere trattato con rispetto e dignità, proprio come te.

(Meh-REHT-tsoh dee eh-SEH-reh trah-TAH-toh kohn ree-SPET-toh eh deeg-nee-TAH, PRO-pree-oh KOH-meh teh)

I understand that we may have different opinions, but that doesn't excuse rude behavior.

Capisco che possiamo avere opinioni diverse, ma ciò non giustifica un comportamento scortese.

(KAH-pee-skoh keh pohs-SEE-amoh ah-VEH-reh oh-pee-NYOH-nee DOOR-veh-seh, mah choh non joo-stee-FEE-kah oon kohm-por-TAH-men-toh skor-TEH-seh)

I don't appreciate being spoken to in that tone.

Non apprezzo di essere parlato con quel tono.

(Non ah-PREHT-tsoh dee EH-seh-reh pahr-LAH-toh kohn kwel TOH-noh)

BEING POLITE

Please
Per favore
(PEHR FAH-voh-reh)

Thank you
Grazie
(GRAHTS-yeh)

Excuse me
Scusi
(SKOO-zee)

I'm sorry
Mi dispiace
(mee dees-pee-AH-cheh)

May I...
Posso...
(POHS-soh...)

Could you...
Potrebbe...
(poh-TREHB-beh...)

Would you...
Vorrebbe...
(vohr-REHB-beh...)

If you don't mind...
Se non gli dispiace...
(seh non lyee dees-pee-AH-cheh...)

With all due respect...
Con tutto il rispetto...
(kohn TOOT-toh eel ree-SPET-toh...)

Pardon me
Mi scusi
(mee SKOO-zee)

After you
Dopo di lei
(DOH-poh dee ley)

Allow me
Mi permetta
(mee per-MEH-tah)

Please, go ahead -
Vada pure
(VAH-dah POOH-reh)

It was my pleasure
È stato un piacere
(eh STAH-toh oon pyah-CHEH-reh)

I appreciate it
Lo apprezzo
(loh ap-PREHT-tsoh)

I'm grateful
Sono grato/a
(SOH-noh GRAH-toh/ah)

That's very kind of you
È molto gentile da parte sua
(eh MOHL-toh JEN-tee-leh dah PAR-teh soo-ah)

I'm honored
Sono onorato/a
(SOH-noh oh-noh-RAH-toh/ah)

I'm flattered
Sono lusingato/a
(SOH-noh loo-zeen-GAH-toh/ah)

I'm obliged
Sono obbligato/a
(SOH-noh oh-BLEE-gah-toh/ah)

If it's not too much trouble
Se non è troppo disturbo
(seh non eh TROHP-poh dee-STOOR-boh)

If you would be so kind
Se fosse così gentile
(seh FOHS-seh koh-SHEE JEN-tee-leh)

If you could spare a moment
Se potesse dedicarmi un momento
(seh poh-TEHS-seh deh-dee-KAHR-mee oon moh-MEN-toh)

If you'll permit me
Se mi permette
(seh mee pehr-MEH-teh)

My apologies
Le mie scuse
(leh MEE-eh SKOO-cheh)

Begging your pardon
Chiedo scusa
(KYEH-doh SKOO-zah)

I beg to differ
Mi permetta di dissentire
(mee per-MEH-tah dee dehs-SEN-teer-reh)

I humbly request
Chiedo umilmente
(KYEH-doh oo-MEEL-men-teh)

I respectfully request
Chiedo con rispetto
(KYEH-doh kohn ree-SPET-toh)

Kindly
Gentilmente
(jen-teeL-MEN-teh)

Sir/Madam
Signore/Signora
(seen-YOH-reh/seen-YOH-rah)

Mr./Ms./Mrs.
Signor/Signora
(seen-YOHR/seen-YOH-rah)

Excuse me, but...
Mi scusi, ma...
(mee SKOO-zee, mah...)

I hate to impose
Mi spiace disturbare
(mee spee-AH-cheh dee-stoor-BAH-reh)

No need to apologize
Non c'è bisogno di scusarsi
(non cheh bee-SOH-nyoh dee skoo-SAHR-see)

That's alright
Va bene
(vah BEH-neh)

I understand
Capisco
(kah-PEES-koh)

Certainly
Certamente
(chehr-tah-MEN-teh)

Absolutely
Assolutamente
(ah-soh-loo-tah-MEN-teh)

You're welcome
Prego
(PREH-goh)

TALKING ABOUT FAMILY

How many people are in your family?
Quante persone ci sono nella tua famiglia?
(KWAHN-teh per-SOH-neh che SO-no nel-la TOO-ah fa-MEEL-yah?)

What's your family like?
Com'è la tua famiglia?
(KOH-meh la TOO-ah fa-MEEL-yah?)

Do you have any siblings?
Hai fratelli o sorelle?
(hai fra-TEL-lee o sor-EL-leh?)

What's your sibling's name?
Come si chiama il tuo fratello o la tua sorella?
(KOH-meh see kee-AH-mah eel TOO-oh fra-TEL-loh o lah TOO-ah sor-EL-lah?)

How old is your sibling?
Quanti anni ha il tuo fratello o la tua sorella?
(KWAN-tee AN-nee ah eel TOO-oh fra-TEL-loh o lah TOO-ah sor-EL-lah?)

Are you close with your siblings?
Sei vicino ai tuoi fratelli o sorelle?
(sey vee-CHEE-noh ah-ee TOO-ee fra-TEL-lee o sor-EL-leh?)

How often do you see your family?
Quanto spesso vedi la tua famiglia?
(KWAN-toh SPESS-soh veh-dee la TOO-ah fa-MEEL-yah?)

What do your parents do for a living?
Cosa fanno i tuoi genitori per vivere?
(KOH-sah FAH-noh ee TOO-ee jen-TOH-ree per vee-VEH-re?)

How did your parents meet?
Come si sono conosciuti i tuoi genitori?
(KOH-meh see SO-no ko-noh-SHOOT-tee ee TOO-ee jeen-TOH-ree?)

Do you have any cousins?
Hai dei cugini?
(hai dei koo-JEE-nee?)

Do you get along well with your cousins?
Ti trovi bene con i tuoi cugini?
(tee TROH-vee BEH-neh kon ee TOO-ee koo-JEE-nee?)

What's your favorite family tradition?
Qual è la tua tradizione di famiglia preferita?
*(kwal eh la TOO-ah tra-dee-TSYOH-neh dee fa-MEEL-yah
pre-feh-REE-tah?)*

What's your favorite family memory?
Qual è il tuo ricordo di famiglia preferito?
(kwal eh eel TOO-oh ree-KOR-do dee fa-MEEL-yah pre-feh-REE-toh?)

Have you ever had a family reunion?
Hai mai partecipato ad un raduno di famiglia?
*(hai mai par-teh-chee-PAH-toh ad oon rah-DOO-noh dee
fa-MEEL-yah?)*

What's your family's cultural background?
Qual è l'origine culturale della tua famiglia?
(kwal eh lor-EE-jee-neh kul-too-RAH-leh del-la TOO-ah fa-MEEL-yah?)

Who's the youngest member of your family?
Chi è il membro più giovane della tua famiglia?
(kee eh eel MEM-broh pyoo jo-VAH-neh del-la TOO-ah fa-MEEL-yah?)

Do you live with your family?
Vivi con la tua famiglia?
(VEE-vee kon la TOO-ah fa-MEEL-yah?)

What's your parents' marriage like?
Com'è il matrimonio dei tuoi genitori?
(KOH-meh eel ma-tri-MO-nyoh dei TOO-ee jen-TOH-ree?)

What's your mother's name?
Come si chiama tua madre?
(KOH-meh see kee-AH-mah TOO-ah MA-dreh?)

What's your father's name?
Come si chiama tuo padre?
(KOH-meh see kee-AH-mah TOO-oh PA-dreh?)

What do your siblings do for a living?
Cosa fanno i tuoi fratelli o sorelle per vivere?
(KOH-sah FAH-noh ee TOO-ee fra-TEL-lee o sor-EL-leh per vee-VEH-re?)

What's your relationship like with your parents?
Com'è il tuo rapporto con i tuoi genitori?
(KOH-meh eel TOO-oh rap-POR-toh kon ee TOO-ee jen-TOH-ree?)

Who's your favorite family member?
Chi è il tuo familiare preferito?
(kee eh eel TOO-oh fa-mee-LYA-reh pre-feh-REE-toh?)

What's your family's favorite hobby?
Qual è il passatempo preferito della tua famiglia?
(kwal eh eel pah-sah-TEM-po pre-feh-REE-toh del-la TOO-ah fa-MEEL-yah?)

Are you similar to anyone in your family?
Sei simile a qualcuno nella tua famiglia?
(sey SEE-mee-leh a kwal-KOO-noh nel-la TOO-ah fa-MEEL-yah?)

Who's the funniest member of your family?
Chi è il membro più divertente della tua famiglia?
(kee eh eel MEM-broh pyoo dee-ver-TEN-teh del-la TOO-ah fa-MEEL-yah?)

Who's the most serious member of your family?
Chi è il membro più serio della tua famiglia?
(kee eh eel MEM-broh pyoo SEH-ree-oh del-la TOO-ah fa-MEEL-yah?)

What's your family's favorite food?
Qual è il cibo preferito della tua famiglia?
(kwal eh eel TCHOH-boh pre-feh-REE-toh del-la TOO-ah fa-MEEL-yah?)

What's your family's favorite holiday?
Qual è la festa preferita della tua famiglia?
(kwal eh lah FEH-sta pre-feh-REE-tah del-la TOO-ah fa-MEEL-yah?)

What's your family's favorite movie?
Qual è il film preferito della tua famiglia?
(kwal eh eel film pre-feh-REE-toh del-la TOO-ah fa-MEEL-yah?)

Who's the most artistic member of your family?
Chi è il membro più artistico della tua famiglia?
(kee eh eel MEM-broh pyoo ar-TEE-stee-koh del-la TOO-ah fa-MEEL-yah?)

Who's the most adventurous member of your family?
Chi è il membro più avventuroso della tua famiglia?
(kee eh eel MEM-broh pyoo av-ven-too-ROH-soh del-la TOO-ah fa-MEEL-yah?)

What's the most memorable family vacation you've been on?
Qual è stata la vacanza in famiglia più memorabile a cui hai partecipato?
(kwal eh STAH-tah lah va-KAN-za een fa-MEE-lya pyoo meh-moh-REE-bleh ah koo-ee ahee par-teh-tsee-PAH-toh?)

What's your family's favorite place to visit?
Qual è il posto preferito della tua famiglia da visitare?
(kwal eh eel PO-stoh pre-feh-REE-toh del-la TOO-ah fa-MEEL-yah dah vee-zee-TAH-reh?)

What's your family's favorite memory?
Qual è il ricordo preferito della tua famiglia?
(kwal eh eel ree-KOR-doh pre-feh-REE-toh del-la TOO-ah fa-MEEL-yah?)

Who's the most hardworking member of your family?
Chi è il membro più lavoratore della tua famiglia?
(kee eh eel MEM-broh pyoo la-vo-RA-toh-reh del-la TOO-ah fa-MEEL-yah?)

What's your family's favorite game to play together?
Qual è il gioco preferito della tua famiglia da giocare insieme?
(kwal eh eel JYO-ko pre-feh-REE-toh del-la TOO-ah fa-MEEL-yah dah jo-KA-reh een-see-EH-meh?)

Who's the most athletic member of your family?
Chi è il membro più atletico della tua famiglia?
(kee eh eel MEM-broh pyoo at-LEH-tee-koh del-la TOO-ah fa-MEEL-yah?)

What's your family's favorite season?
Qual è la stagione preferita della tua famiglia?
(kwal eh lah sta-JO-neh pre-feh-REE-tah del-la TOO-ah fa-MEEL-yah?)

What's your family's favorite holiday tradition?
Qual è la tradizione festiva preferita della tua famiglia?
(kwal eh lah tra-dee-TSYO-neh fes-TEE-vah pre-feh-REE-tah del-la TOO-ah fa-MEEL-yah?)

MAKING SUGGESTIONS

Have you considered trying...?
Avete considerato di provare...?
(ah-VEH-teh kohn-si-de-RA-toh dee PRO-va-reh)

Why don't we...?
Perché non...?
(PEHR-keh nohn)

How about...?
Che ne dite di...?
(keh neh DEE-teh dee)

Maybe we could...?
Forse potremmo...?
(FOR-seh poh-TREHM-moh)

I think it would be a good idea to...
Penso che sarebbe una buona idea...
(PEN-soh keh sah-REH-bee-eh OO-nah BWOH-nah EE-deh-ah)

What if we...?
E se noi...?
(EH seh NOH-ee)

I suggest that we...
Suggerisco che noi...
(sood-jeh-RIH-skoh keh NOH-ee)

Would you like to try...?
Vorresti provare...?
(voh-RES-tee pro-VA-reh)

Let's try...
Proviamo...
(pro-VEE-ah-moh)

It might be worth considering...
Potrebbe valere la pena considerare...
(poh-TREHB-beh VAH-leh-reh lah PEH-nah kohn-si-deh-RAH-reh)

EXPRESSING OPINIONS

In my opinion...
A mio parere...
(ah MEE-o pah-RAY-reh)

From my point of view...
Dal mio punto di vista...
(dahl MEE-o POON-toh dee VEE-stah)

As far as I'm concerned...
Per quanto mi riguarda...
(pair KWOHN-toh mee ree-GWAR-dah)

I believe that...
Credo che...
(KRAY-doh keh...)

Personally, I think that...
Personalmente, penso che...
(pehr-soh-nahl-MEN-teh, PEN-soh keh...)

It seems to me that...
Mi sembra che...
(mee SEM-bra keh...)

I feel that...
Sento che...
(SEN-toh keh...)

I am convinced that...
Sono convinto/a che...
(SOH-noh kohn-VEEN-toh/ah keh...)

To my mind...
Secondo me...
(seh-KOHN-doh meh...)

I would argue that...
Argomenterei che...
(ar-goh-men-teh-REH-ee keh...)

It's my belief that...
È la mia convinzione che...
(eh lah MEE-ah kohn-veen-TSYOH-neh keh...)

As I see it...
Come la vedo io...
(KO-meh lah VEH-doh ee-oh...)

The way I see it...
Il modo in cui lo vedo io...
(eel MOH-doh een KOO-ee loh VEH-doh ee-oh...)

GIVING AND ASKING FOR ADVICE

Can I ask your opinion on something?
Posso chiederti il tuo parere su qualcosa?
(POSS-oh kee-eh-DEHR-tee eel TOO-oh pah-REH-reh soo koo-AHL-koh-sah?)

What do you think I should do?
Cosa pensi che dovrei fare?
(KOH-sah PEHN-see keh DOH-vreh-ee FAH-reh?)

I'm at a crossroads and need some advice, what do you suggest?
Sono a un bivio e ho bisogno di un consiglio, cosa suggerisci?
(SOH-noh ah oon BEE-vee-oh eh oh bee-SOH-nyoh dee oon kohn-SEE-lyoh, KOH-sah soog-JEH-ree-shee?)

Could you help me with a decision?
Potresti aiutarmi a prendere una decisione?
(poh-TREH-stee ah-yoo-TAHR-mee ah prehn-DEH-reh OO-nah dee-zyoh-NEH-tseh?)

What's your take on this situation?
Qual è il tuo punto di vista su questa situazione?
(kwahl eh eel TOO-oh POON-toh dee VEE-stah soo KWEHS-tah soo-tyoo-AH-tsee-OH-neh?)

Do you have any advice for me?
Hai qualche consiglio da darmi?
(AI KWEHL-keh kohn-SEE-lyoh dah DAHR-mee?)

I'm struggling with something and could use your advice, can you help?
Sto lottando con qualcosa e potrei usare il tuo consiglio, puoi aiutarmi?
(stoh loh-TAHN-doh kohn kwahl-KOH-sah eh poh-TREH-ee oo-SAH-reh eel TOO-oh kohn-SEE-lyoh, pwoh-ee ah-yoo-TAHR-mee?)

What would you do if you were in my shoes?
Cosa faresti se fossi al mio posto?
(KOH-sah fah-REH-stee seh FOH-see ahl MEE-oh POH-stoh?)

Do you have any suggestions for me?
Hai qualche suggerimento da darmi?
(AI KWEHL-keh soo-jeh-REE-men-toh dah DAHR-mee?)

How would you handle this?
Come gestiresti questa situazione?
(KOH-meh je-STEE-reh-stee KWEHS-tah soo-tyoo-AH-tsee-OH-neh?)

Can you give me your perspective on this?
Puoi darmi la tua prospettiva su questa cosa?
(pwoh-ee DAHR-mee lah TOO-ah proh-speh-TTEE-vah soo KWEHS-tah KOH-zah?)

I need some guidance, can you offer some advice?
Ho bisogno di una guida, puoi darmi qualche consiglio?
(oh bee-SOH-nyoh dee OO-nah GWEE-dah, pwoh-ee DAHR-mee KWEHL-keh kohn-SEE-lyoh?)

I'm not sure what to do, can you give me some advice?
Non sono sicuro di cosa fare, puoi darmi qualche consiglio?
(non SOH-noh see-KOO-roh dee KOH-sah FAH-reh, pwoh-ee DAHR-mee KWEHL-keh kohn-SEE-lyoh?)

How should I handle this?
Come dovrei gestire questa situazione?
(KOH-meh doh-VREH-ee je-STEE-reh KWEHS-tah soo-tyoo-AH-tsee-OH-neh?)

What's your recommendation?
Qual è il tuo consiglio?
(kwahl eh eel TOO-oh kohn-SEE-lyoh?)

Can you give me some feedback on this idea?
Puoi darmi un feedback su questa idea?
(pwoh-ee DAHR-mee oon FEE-deh-bahk soo KWEHS-tah EE-dee-ah?)

I'm having trouble deciding, what would you suggest?
Sto avendo difficoltà a decidere, cosa suggeriresti?
(stoh ah-VEHN-doh dee-fee-KOHL-tee ah deh-CHEE-deh-reh, KOH-sah soog-JEH-ree-res-tee?)

Do you think this is a good idea?
Pensi che sia una buona idea?
(PEHN-see keh see-yah OO-nah BWOH-nah EE-dee-ah?)

Can you give me some input on this matter?
Puoi darmi qualche suggerimento su questa questione?
(pwoh-ee DAHR-mee KWEHL-keh soo-jeh-REE-men-too soo KWEHS-tyoh-neh?)

What's your advice?
Qual è il tuo consiglio?
(kwahl eh eel TOO-oh kohn-SEE-lyoh?)

I need your advice, can you help me out?
Ho bisogno del tuo consiglio, puoi aiutarmi?
(oh bee-SOH-nyoh dehl TOO-oh kohn-SEE-lyoh, pwoh-ee ah-yoo-TAHR-mee?)

Can you give me some pointers on this issue?
Puoi darmi alcuni suggerimenti su questa questione?
(pwoh-ee DAHR-mee ahl-KOO-nee soo-jeh-REE-men-tee soo KWEHS-tyoh-neh?)

I'm seeking your guidance, what do you suggest?
Sto cercando la tua guida, cosa suggerisci?
(stoh cher-KAHN-doh lah TOO-ah GWEE-dah, KOH-sah soog-JEH-ree-shee?)

What's your take on this matter?
Qual è il tuo punto di vista su questa questione?
(kwahl eh eel TOO-oh POON-toh dee VEE-stah soo KWEHS-tyoh-neh?)

Could you offer me some advice?
Potresti offrirmi un consiglio?
(poh-TREH-stee ohf-FEER-mee oon kohn-SEE-lyoh?)

I'm not sure what to do, can you give me your opinion?
Non so cosa fare, puoi darmi il tuo parere?
*(non soh KOH-sah FAH-reh, pwoh-ee DAHR-mee eel TOO-oh
pah-REH-reh?)*

What would you do if you were in my situation?
Cosa faresti se fossi al mio posto?
(KOH-sah fahr-EH-stee seh FOH-see ahl MEE-oh POH-stoh?)

Can you help me make a decision?
Puoi aiutarmi a prendere una decisione?
*(pwoh-ee ah-yoo-TAHR-mee ah prehn-DEH-reh OO-nah
dee-chee-ZYO-neh?)*

What do you think I should do?
Cosa pensi che dovrei fare?
(KOH-sah PEHN-see keh doh-VREH-ee FAH-reh?)

I need your opinion on this matter
Ho bisogno del tuo parere su questa questione
(oh bee-SOH-nyoh dehl TOO-oh pah-REH-reh soo KWEHS-tyoh-neh)

Do you have any suggestions for me?
Hai qualche suggerimento per me?
(AI KWAHL-keh soo-jeh-REE-men-toh pehr meh?)

I'm torn between two options, what do you think?
Sono indeciso tra due opzioni, cosa ne pensi?
*(SOH-noh een-deh-CHEE-zoh trah DOO-eh ohp-zee-OH-nee, KOH-sah
neh PEHN-see?)*

I don't know what to do next, can you advise me?
Non so cosa fare dopo, puoi consigliarmi?
(non soh KOH-sah FAH-reh DOH-poh, pwoh-ee kohn-see-LYAR-mee?)

What's your view on this matter?
Qual è la tua opinione su questa questione?
(KWAH-leh lah TOO-ah oh-pee-NYOH-neh soo KWEHS-tyoh-neh?)

Can you guide me in the right direction?
Puoi guidarmi nella giusta direzione?
(pwoh-ee GWEE-dahr-mee neh-lah JYOO-stah dee-reh-TSYOH-neh?)

I'm at a loss, what should I do?
Sono in difficoltà, cosa dovrei fare?
(SOH-noh een dee-fee-KOHL-tah, KOH-sah doh-VREH-ee FAH-reh?)

I need your help, what do you suggest?
Ho bisogno del tuo aiuto, cosa suggerisci?
(oh bee-SOH-nyoh dehl TOO-oh ah-YOO-toh, KOH-sah soog-JEH-ree-shee?)

Can you give me some tips on how to handle this?
Puoi darmi dei suggerimenti su come gestire questa situazione?
(pwoh-ee DAHR-mee deh-ee soo-jeh-REE-men-tee soo KOH-meh je-STEE-reh KWEHS-tah soo-tyoo-AH-tsee-OH-neh?)

What do you think is the best course of action for me?
Qual è, secondo te, il miglior corso di azione per me?
(KWAH-leh eh, seh-GOHN-doh teh, eel mee-lyohr KOHR-soh dee ah-TSYOH-neh pehr meh?)

I'm not sure which option is better, can you help me weigh the pros and cons?
Non sono sicuro quale opzione sia migliore, puoi aiutarmi a valutare i pro e i contro?
(non SO-noh see-KOO-roh KWAH-leh ohp-ZYO-neh see-ah meel-YOH-reh, pwoh-ee ah-yoo-TAHR-mee ah vah-LOO-tah-reh ee proh eh ee KON-troh?)

TALKING ABOUT LIKES AND DISLIKES

I love pizza.
Amo la pizza.
(AH-moh lah PEET-tsah)

I really enjoy listening to music.
Mi piace molto ascoltare la musica.
(mee pee-AH-cheh MOHL-toh ah-skohl-TAH-reh lah moo-SEE-kah)

I'm a big fan of horror movies.
Sono un grande appassionato di film dell'orrore.
(SOH-noh oon GRAHN-deh ah-pahs-see-oh-NAH-toh dee feelm dell-OH-roh-reh)

I adore spending time with my family.
Adoro trascorrere del tempo con la mia famiglia.
(ah-DOH-roh trah-SKOR-reh dehl TEM-poh kohn lah MEE-ah fah-MEE-lyah)

I'm crazy about chocolate.
Sono pazzo per il cioccolato.
(SOH-noh PAT-tso pehr eel chohk-ko-LAH-toh)

I'm passionate about playing sports.
Sono appassionato di giocare a sport.
(SOH-noh ah-pahs-see-oh-NAH-toh dee joh-KAH-reh ah sport)

I'm fond of reading novels.
Mi piace leggere romanzi.
(mee pee-AH-cheh leh-JEH-reh roh-MAHN-tsee)

I'm addicted to watching TV shows.
Sono dipendente dalla visione di serie tv.
(SOH-noh dee-pehn-DEN-teh DAHL-lah vee-ZYOH-neh dee SEH-ryeh TV)

I can't get enough of traveling.
Non mi sazio mai di viaggiare.
(non mee SAH-tsee-oh mah-ee dee vee-ah-JJAH-reh)

I'm keen on learning new languages.
Sono interessato a imparare nuove lingue.
(SOH-noh een-teh-RES-sah-toh ah eem-PAH-reh NOO-veh LEE-nyoo-eh)

I'm really into photography.
Mi piace molto la fotografia.
(mee pee-AH-cheh MOHL-toh lah foh-toh-GRAH-fee-ah)

I'm fascinated by history.
Sono affascinato dalla storia.
(SOH-noh ahf-fah-shee-NAH-toh DAHL-lah STOH-ryah)

I'm obsessed with fashion.
Sono ossessionato dalla moda.
(SOH-noh os-sehss-see-OH-nah-toh DAHL-lah MOH-dah)

I'm a huge fan of Harry Potter.
Sono un grande fan di Harry Potter.
(SOH-noh oon GRAHN-deh fahn dee HAH-ree POHT-tehr)

I'm really passionate about cooking.
Sono appassionato di cucinare.
(SOH-noh ah-pahs-see-oh-NAH-toh dee koo-chee-NAH-reh)

I love going to the beach.
Amo andare in spiaggia.
(AH-moh ahn-DAH-reh een SPYAH-jah)

I enjoy hiking in the mountains.
Mi piace fare escursioni in montagna.
(mee pee-AH-cheh FAH-reh eh-skoor-see-OH-nee een mohn-TAH-nyah)

I'm fond of eating sushi.
Mi piace mangiare il sushi.
(mee pee-AH-cheh mahn-jah-REH eel SOO-shee)

I love playing video games.
Amo giocare ai videogiochi.
(AH-moh joh-KAH-reh ah-ee vee-dee-oh-JOH-kee)

I'm crazy about ice cream.
Sono pazzo per il gelato.
(SOH-noh PAT-tso pehr eel jeh-LAH-toh)

I'm really into art.
Mi interessa molto l'arte.
(mee een-teh-RES-sah MOHL-toh LAHR-teh)

I'm a big fan of science fiction movies.
Sono un grande appassionato di film di fantascienza.
(SOH-noh oon GRAHN-deh ah-pahs-see-oh-NAH-toh dee feelm dee fahn-tah-SHYEH-nzah)

I enjoy dancing.
Mi piace ballare.
(mee pee-AH-cheh bah-LAH-reh)

I love going to concerts.
Amo andare ai concerti.
(AH-moh ahn-DAH-reh ah-ee kohn-CHER-tee)

I hate spiders.
Odio i ragni.
(OH-dee-oh ee RAH-nyee)

I can't stand seafood.
Non sopporto i frutti di mare.
(non soh-POHR-toh ee FROO-tee dee MAH-reh)

I'm not a fan of horror movies.
Non sono un appassionato di film dell'orrore.
(non SOH-noh oon ah-pahs-see-oh-NAH-toh dee feelm dell-OH-roh-reh)

I don't like spicy food.
Non mi piace il cibo piccante.
(non mee pee-AH-cheh eel CHEE-boh pee-KAHN-teh)

I'm not interested in politics.
Non mi interessa la politica.
(non mee een-teh-RES-sah lah poh-LEE-tee-kah)

I don't enjoy watching sports.
Non mi piace guardare gli sport.
(non mee pee-AH-cheh gwar-DAH-reh lyee sport)

I can't stand loud music.
Non sopporto la musica forte.
(non soh-POHR-toh lah moo-SEE-kah FOHR-teh)

I'm not a fan of romantic comedies.
Non sono un appassionato di commedie romantiche.
(non SOH-noh oon ah-pahs-see-oh-NAH-toh dee kohm-MEH-dee roh-mahn-TIH-keh)

I hate public speaking.
Odio parlare in pubblico.
(OH-dee-oh pahr-LAH-reh een POOB-blee-koh)

I don't like driving in traffic.
Non mi piace guidare nel traffico.
(non mee pee-AH-cheh gwee-DAH-reh nehl TRAF-fee-koh)

I dislike cleaning the house.
Non mi piace pulire la casa.
(non mee pee-AH-cheh poo-LEE-reh lah KAH-sah)

I can't stand waiting in line.
Non sopporto aspettare in fila.
(non soh-POHR-toh ahs-peh-TAH-reh een FEE-lah)

I'm not a fan of spicy food.
Non sono un appassionato di cibo piccante.
(non SOH-noh oon ah-pahs-see-oh-NAH-toh dee CHEE-boh pee-KAHN-teh)

I hate being late.
Odio essere in ritardo.
(OH-dee-oh EHSS-eh-reh een ree-TAR-doh)

I don't like cold weather.
Non mi piace il tempo freddo.
(non mee pee-AH-cheh eel TEHM-poh FREHD-doh)

I'm not a fan of horror novels.
Non sono un appassionato di romanzi dell'orrore.
(non SOH-noh oon ah-pahs-see-oh-NAH-toh dee roh-MAHN-tsee dell-OH-roh-reh)

EXPRESSING AGREEMENT AND DISAGREEMENT

I completely agree.
Io sono completamente d'accordo.
(EE-o so-no com-ple-ta-MEN-te da-KOR-do)

That's exactly what I was thinking.
Esattamente quello che stavo pensando.
(E-sat-TA-men-te KWE-llo ke STAvoh pen-SAN-do)

You're right.
Hai ragione.
(AI ra-GIO-ne)

I couldn't agree more.
Non potrei essere più d'accordo.
(Non po-TRE-i es-SE-re più da-KOR-do)

Absolutely.
Assolutamente.
(As-so-lu-ta-MEN-te)

Precisely.
Esattamente.
(E-sat-TA-men-te)

I see eye to eye with you on this.
Siamo sulla stessa lunghezza d'onda su questo.
(SIAM-o sul-la STES-sa LUN-ghez-za don-da su KWE-sto)

You hit the nail on the head.
Hai centrato il punto.
(AI cen-TRA-to il PUN-to)

I concur.
Concordo.
(Con-COR-do)

You have a valid point there.
Hai un punto valido lì.
(AI un PUN-to va-LI-do li)

That's a good point.
È un buon punto.
(È un buon PUN-to)

I'm with you on that one.
Sono d'accordo con te su questo.
(SO-no da-KOR-do con TE su KWE-sto)

You're spot on.
Hai colto nel segno.
(AI COL-to nel SEG-no)

I couldn't have said it better myself.
Non avrei potuto dirlo meglio io stesso.
(Non a-VRE-i po-TU-to DIR-lo meg-LIO io STES-so)

I'm in total agreement.
Sono completamente d'accordo.
(SO-no com-ple-ta-MEN-te da-KOR-do)

I'm on board with that.
Sono d'accordo con questo.
(SO-no da-KOR-do con KWE-sto)

That's true.
È vero.
(È VE-ro)

That's exactly how I feel.
È esattamente come mi sento.
(È E-sat-TA-men-te KO-me mi SEN-to)

You've convinced me.
Mi hai convinto.
(Mi hai con-VIN-to)

I fully support your idea/opinion.
Sostengo completamente la tua idea/opinione.
(So-STEN-go com-ple-ta-MEN-te la tua i-DE-a/o-pi-NIO-ne)

I agree wholeheartedly.
Sono pienamente d'accordo.
(SO-no pie-NA-men-te da-KOR-do)

That's a fair assessment.
È una valutazione equa.
(È u-na va-lu-ta-ZIO-ne e-KWA)

I'm glad you brought that up.
Sono contento che tu abbia portato questo in discussione.
(SO-no con-TEN-to ke tu AB-bia por-TA-to KWE-sto in dis-KUS-sio-ne)

You make a compelling argument.
Fai un argomento convincente.
(FAI un ar-go-MEN-to con-VIN-tsen-te)

I see your point.
Capisco il tuo punto di vista.
(KA-pis-ko il tuo PUN-to di VI-sta)

I'm sorry, but I don't agree with you.
Mi dispiace, ma non sono d'accordo con te.
(Mi dis-PIA-ce, ma non SO-no da-KOR-do con TE)

I'm afraid I have to disagree with you.
Mi spiace, ma devo dissentire da te.
(Mi spi-A-ce, ma DE-vo dis-SAN-ti-re da TE)

I don't see it that way.
Io non la penso così.
(Io non la PEN-so CO-sì)

I'm not so sure about that.
Non ne sono così sicuro.
(Non ne SO-no co-SÌ si-CU-ro)

I beg to differ.
Mi permetto di dissentire.
(Mi per-MET-to di dis-SAN-ti-re)

That's not entirely true.
Non è del tutto vero.
(Non è del TOT-to VE-ro)

I'm sorry, but I must disagree.
Mi dispiace, ma devo dissentire.
(Mi dis-PIA-ce, ma DE-vo dis-SAN-ti-re)

I can't say that I agree with you.
Non posso dire di essere d'accordo con te.
(Non PO-sso DI-re di es-SE-re da-KOR-do con TE)

I see things differently.
Io la vedo diversamente.
(Io la VE-do di-ver-sa-MEN-te)

I'm sorry, but that's not how I see it.
Mi dispiace, ma non la penso così.
(Mi dis-PIA-ce, ma non la PEN-so CO-sì)

I don't think that's quite right.
Non penso che sia del tutto corretto.
(Non PEN-so ke SIA del TOT-to co-RET-to)

I have a different point of view.
Ho un punto di vista diverso.
(Ho un PUN-to di VI-sta di-VER-so)

I'm not convinced.
Non sono convinto.
(Non SO-no con-VIN-to)

That's not how I understand it.
Non è così che lo capisco.
(Non è CO-sì ke lo ca-PIS-co)

I respectfully disagree.
Non sono d'accordo con rispetto.
(Non SO-no da-KOR-do con ri-SPE-to)

MAKING EXCUSES

I'm sorry, I'm running late because of traffic.
Mi dispiace, sono in ritardo a-CAU-sa del traffi-co.
(mee dee-SPYA-che, SO-no in ree-TAR-do a-COW-sa del TRAF-fi-co)

I had an emergency to take care of.
Ho avuto un'emergenza da risolvere.
(o a-VOO-to oon-e-mer-DJEN-za da ree-SOL-ve-re)

I apologize for not meeting the deadline; I had unforeseen circumstances.
Mi scuso per non aver rispettato la scadenza; ho avuto circostanze impreviste.
(mee SKOO-zo per non a-ver ree-spe-TA-to la ska-DEN-za; o a-VOO-to chir-ko-STAN-tse im-pre-VIS-te)

I couldn't make it because I had a family obligation.
Non ho potuto esserci a causa di un impegno familiare.
(non o po-TOO-to es-SER-tsi a-KAU-sa di oon im-PEN-yo fa-mee-LYA-re)

I'm sorry; I forgot to set my alarm.
Mi dispiace; ho dimenticato di impostare la sveglia.
(mee dee-SPYA-che; o dee-men-tee-KA-to di im-pos-TA-re la sve-GLYA)

I had a doctor's appointment that took longer than expected.
Ho avuto un appuntamento dal dottore che è durato più del previsto.
(o a-VOO-to oon ap-poon-ta-MEN-to dal dot-TO-re ke è du-RA-to pjo del pre-VIS-to)

I'm sorry; I had a flat tire on the way here.
Mi dispiace; ho avuto una gomma a terra sulla strada.
(mee dee-SPYA-che; o a-VOO-to oo-na GOM-ma a TERRA sul-la STRA-da)

I apologize for not being able to attend; I'm feeling under the weather.
Mi scuso per non poter partecipare; non mi sento bene.
(mee SKOO-zo per non po-TARE par-te-chee-PA-re; non mee SEN-to BE-ne)

I'm sorry; I have a prior engagement that I cannot miss.
Mi dispiace; ho un impegno precedente che non posso mancare.
(mee dee-SPYA-che; o oon im-PEN-yo pre-che-DEN-te ke non PO-so man-KA-re)

I couldn't make it because of a scheduling conflict.
Non ho potuto esserci a causa di un conflitto di programmazione.
(non o po-TOO-to es-SER-tsi a-KAU-sa di oon kon-FLIT-to di pro-gram-MA-tse-o-nee)

I apologize; I was unaware of the time change.
Mi scuso; non sapevo del cambio di orario.
(mee SKOO-zo; non sa-PE-vo del CAM-byo di o-RA-ryo)

I couldn't make it because my car broke down.
Non ho potuto esserci perché la mia macchina si è guastata.
(non o po-TOO-to es-SER-tsi per-KAY la MEE-a MA-kkee-na see e gwaa-STAA-ta)

I'm sorry, but I have a family emergency to attend to.
Mi dispiace, ma ho un'emergenza familiare da affrontare.
(mee dee-SPYA-che, ma o oon-e-mer-DJEN-za fa-mee-LYA-re da af-fron-TA-re)

I apologize; I'm dealing with some personal issues right now.
Mi scuso; sto affrontando alcune questioni personali al momento.
(mee SKOO-zo; sto af-fron-TAN-do al-KOO-ne kwiązń per-so-NA-li al mo-MEN-to)

I'm sorry; I got lost on the way here.
Mi dispiace; mi sono perso per strada.
(mee dee-SPYA-che; mee SO-no PER-so per STRA-da)

I couldn't make it because of a family commitment.
Non ho potuto esserci a causa di un impegno familiare.
(non o po-TOO-to es-SER-tsi a-KAU-sa di oon im-PEN-yo fa-mee-LYA-re)

I'm sorry, but I'm not feeling well.
Mi dispiace, ma non mi sento bene.
(mee dee-SPYA-che, ma non mee SEN-to BE-ne)

I couldn't make it because of transportation issues.
Non ho potuto esserci a causa di problemi di trasporto.
(non o po-TOO-to es-SER-tsi a-KAU-sa di pro-BLE-mee dee TRAS-por-to)

I'm sorry; I had to take care of a personal matter.
Mi dispiace; ho dovuto occuparmi di una questione personale.
*(mee dee-SPYA-che; o do-VU-to ok-koo-par-mi di oona kwiązń
per-so-NA-le)*

I couldn't make it because of a work-related emergency.
Non ho potuto esserci a causa di un'emergenza legata al lavoro.
*(non o po-TOO-to es-SER-tsi a-KAU-sa di oon-e-mer-DJEN-za le-GA-ta al
la-VO-ro)*

I'm sorry, but I have a prior commitment.
Mi dispiace, ma ho un impegno precedente.
(mee dee-SPYA-che, ma o oon im-PEN-yo pre-che-DEN-te)

I couldn't make it because of an illness.
Non ho potuto esserci a causa di una malattia.
(non o po-TOO-to es-SER-tsi a-KAU-sa dee oo-na ma-LAT-tya)

I'm sorry, but I have a family obligation that cannot be postponed.
Mi dispiace, ma ho un impegno familiare che non può essere
rimandato.
*(mee dee-SPYA-che, ma o oon im-PEN-yo fa-mee-LYA-re ke non
pwo-Es-se ree-MAN-da-to)*

I couldn't make it because of an unexpected event.
Non ho potuto esserci a causa di un evento imprevisto.
(non o po-TOO-to es-SER-tsi a-KAU-sa di oon even-to im-pre-VI-sto)

I'm sorry, but I have a conflicting engagement.
Mi dispiace, ma ho un impegno in conflitto.
(mee dee-SPYA-che, ma o oon im-PEN-yo een kon-FLIT-to)

I couldn't make it because I'm out of town.
Non ho potuto esserci perché sono fuori città.
(non o po-TOO-to es-SER-tsi per-KAY SO-no FWO-ree che-ta)

I'm sorry, but I have a prior engagement.
Mi dispiace, ma ho un impegno precedente.
(mee dee-SPYA-che, ma o oon im-PEN-yo pre-che-DEN-te)

I couldn't make it because I have a conflicting appointment.
Non ho potuto esserci perché ho un appuntamento in conflitto.
(non o po-TOO-to es-SER-tsi per-KAY o oon ap-poon-ta-MEN-to een kon-FLIT-to)

I'm sorry, but I have an important personal matter to attend to.
Mi dispiace, ma ho una questione personale importante da affrontare.
(mee dee-SPYA-che, ma o oo-na kwiązń per-so-NA-le eem-por-TAN-te da af-fron-TA-re)

I couldn't make it because of a last-minute emergency.
Non ho potuto esserci a causa di un'emergenza dell'ultimo minuto.
(non o po-TOO-to es-SER-tsi a-KAU-sa di oon-e-mer-DJEN-za dell-ool-TEE-mo mee-NOO-to)

I'm sorry, but I'm double-booked.
Mi dispiace, ma ho un doppio impegno.
(mee dee-SPYA-che, ma o oon DOP-pyo im-PEN-yo)

I couldn't make it because of a scheduling conflict.
Non ho potuto esserci a causa di un conflitto di programmazione.
(non o po-TOO-to es-SER-tsi a-KAU-sa di oon kon-FLIT-to dee pro-gram-MA-tsyo-nee)

I'm sorry, but I have a work-related commitment.
Mi dispiace, ma ho un impegno legato al lavoro.
(mee dee-SPYA-che, ma o oon im-PEN-yo le-GA-to al la-VO-ro)

I couldn't make it because I have a family function to attend.

Non ho potuto esserci perché ho una funzione familiare a cui partecipare.

(non o po-TOO-to es-SER-tsi per-KAY o oo-na FOON-tsyo-nee fa-mee-LYA-re a koo-ee par-te-CHEE-pa-re)

I'm sorry, but I have a conflicting personal matter to attend to.

Mi dispiace, ma ho una questione personale in conflitto da affrontare.

(mee dee-SPYA-che, ma o oo-na kwiązń per-so-NA-le een kon-FLIT-to da af-fron-TA-re)

I'm sorry, but I have a medical appointment.

Mi dispiace, ma ho un appuntamento medico.

(mee dee-SPYA-che, ma o oon ap-poon-ta-MEN-to ME-di-ko)

I couldn't make it because I have a prior family commitment.

Non ho potuto esserci perché ho un impegno familiare precedente.

(non o po-TOO-to es-SER-tsi per-KAY o oon im-PEN-yo fa-mee-LYA-re pre-che-DEN-te)

I'm sorry, but I have a prior engagement with friends.

Mi dispiace, ma ho un impegno precedente con gli amici.

(mee dee-SPYA-che, ma o oon im-PEN-yo pre-che-DEN-te kon ly a-MEE-chee)

I couldn't make it because of transportation issues.

Non ho potuto esserci a causa di problemi di trasporto.

(non o po-TOO-to es-SER-tsi a-KAU-sa di pro-BLE-mee dee tra-SPOR-to)

I'm sorry, but I have a deadline to meet.

Mi dispiace, ma ho una scadenza da rispettare.

(mee dee-SPYA-che, ma o oo-na ska-DEN-tsa da ri-spe-TTA-re)

ASKING AND GIVING PERMISSION

Can I ask you something?
Posso chiedertI qualcosa?
(POS-so kye-der-TEE kwa-LO-sa)

Do you mind if I take a break?
TI dispiace se faccio una pausa?
(tee di-SPYA-tche se FATCH-eeo OO-na POW-za)

Would it be okay if I left early today?
Sarebbe ok se partissi prima oggi?
(sa-REB-be OK se par-TEE-see PREE-ma OJ-ji)

May I borrow your pencil?
Posso prendere in prestitto la tua matita?
(POS-so pren-DE-re in pre-STEE-to la TOO-a ma-TEE-ta)

Is it alright if I use the restroom?
Va bene se uso il bagno?
(va BE-ne se OO-so il BAN-yo)

Could I have a glass of water, please?
Potrei avere un bicchiere d'acqua, per favore?
(po-TREI a-VE-re oon beek-KYEH-re DA-kwa per fa-VO-re)

Would you mind if I turned up the air conditioning?
Ti dispiace se alzo l'aria condizionata?
(tee di-SPYA-tche se AL-tso LA-ria kon-di-TSYO-na-ta)

Do you give me permission to share this information?
Mi dai il permesso di condividere queste informazioni?
(mi DA-i il per-MES-so di kon-dee-VEE-de-re KWE-ste in-for-ma-TSYO-nee)

Would it be okay if I made a suggestion?
Sarebbe ok se facessi una suggerimento?
(sa-REB-be OK se FA-ches-see OO-na SOO-jhe-ree-MEN-to)

May I use your phone?
Posso usare il tuo cellulare?
(POS-so oo-SA-re il TOO-o che-LOO-lah-re)

Can I borrow your car tonight?
Posso prendere in prestito la tua macchina stasera?
(POS-so pren-DE-re in pre-STEE-to la TOO-a ma-KY-na sta-SE-ra)

Do you mind if I close the window?
TI dispiace se chiudo la finestra?
(tee di-SPYA-tche se KYOO-do la fee-NEES-tra)

Would it be okay if I took a picture?
Sarebbe ok se facessi una fotografia?
(sa-REB-be OK se FA-ches-see OO-na fo-to-GRA-fya)

May I ask you to repeat that?
Posso chiederti di ripetere?
(POS-so kyeh-DEER-tee di ree-pe-TE-re)

Could I have your permission to publish this article?
Potrei avere il tuo permesso per pubblicare questo articolo?
(po-TREI a-VE-re il TOO-o per-MES-so per POOB-bli-ka-re KWES-to ar-TEE-ko-lo)

Can I smoke here?
Posso fumare qui?
(POS-so foo-MA-re kwee?)

Do you mind if I turn off the TV?
Ti dispiace se spegno la tv?
(tee di-SPYA-tche se SPE-nyo la TV?)

Would it be okay if I bring my dog to the park?
Sarebbe ok se portassi il mio cane al parco?
(sa-REB-be OK se POR-TAS-see il MEE-o KA-ne al PAR-ko?)

May I leave early for a doctor's appointment?
Posso andare via prima per un'appuntamento dal dottore?
(POS-so an-DA-re VYA PREE-ma per oon ap-poon-ta-MEN-to dal dot-TO-re?)

Sure, go ahead!
Certo, vai avanti!
(CHEHR-to, VA-ee a-VAN-tee!)

Of course, you can!
Certo, puoi farlo!
(CHEHR-to, PWOY FAR-lo!)

Yes, feel free to do that.
Sì, sentiti libero di farlo.
(SEE, sen-TEE-tee LYE-beh-roh dee FAR-loh.)

Absolutely, go for it!
Assolutamente, fallo!
(A-soo-loo-ta-MEN-te, FA-loh!)

You have my permission.
Hai il mio permesso.
(HI il MEE-o per-MES-so.)

I don't see why not.
Non vedo perché no.
(NON VEH-do pehr-KAY no.)

By all means, please do.
Fai pure, per favore.
(FAI PU-reh, per fa-VO-re.)

It's fine with me.
Va bene per me.
(VA BEH-neh per meh.)

You are welcome to do that.
Sei il benvenuto a farlo.
(SEH-ee il ben-VEH-noo-toh a FAR-loh.)

I don't mind at all.
Non mi dispiace per niente.
(NON mee di-SPYA-cheh per NYEN-teh.)

That's no problem at all.
Non c'è nessun problema.
(NON cheh NEH-soon pro-BLE-mah.)

Be my guest.
Facci pure.
(FAT-chee PU-reh.)

I give you my blessing.
Ti do la mia benedizione.
(TEE doh lah MEE-a ben-eh-dee-TSYO-neh.)

It's perfectly fine.
È perfettamente ok.
(EH per-feht-ta-MEN-teh OK.)

You have my consent.
Hai il mio consenso.
(HI il MEE-o kon-SEN-so.)

I authorize you to do that.
Ti autorizzo a farlo.
(TEE aw-toh-REE-tsoh a FAR-loh.)

Don't hesitate to do it.
Non esitare a farlo.
(NON eh-see-TA-reh a FAR-loh.)

It's okay with me.
Va bene per me.
(VA BEH-neh per meh.)

172

That's perfectly fine with me.
Non c'è problema per me.
(NON cheh pro-BLE-mah per meh.)

You are permitted to do that.
Ti è permesso farlo.
(TEE eh per-MES-soh FAR-loh.)

You are cleared to proceed.
Puoi procedere, sei autorizzato.
(PWOY pro-che-DEH-reh, SEH-ee aw-toh-REE-tsa-toh.)

BUSINESS NEGOTIATION

Can we start by discussing the terms of the agreement?
Posiamo cominciare discutendo i termini dell'accordo?
(PO-ssi-amo ko-MIN-tsa-re dis-KU-ten-do i TER-mi dell-a-KKOR-do?)

What are your expectations for this partnership?
Quali sono le tue aspettative per questa partnership?
(KWA-li SO-no le TU-e as-pe-TA-ti-ve per KWE-sta part-ner-SHIP?)

Could you please clarify your proposal?
Potresti per favore chiarire la tua proposta?
(PO-tres-ti per fa-VO-re kja-RI-re la TU-a pro-PO-sta?)

Let's go over the details of the contract.
Andiamo sui dettagli del contratto.
(AN-dja-mo sui DET-ta-GLI del kon-TRAT-to.)

How can we ensure mutual benefits in this deal?
Come possiamo assicurare benefici reciproci in questo accordo?
(KO-me POS-sia-mo as-si-ku-RA-re be-ne-fi-tsi re-ko-PRI-tsi in KWE-sto ak-KOR-do?)

Can you provide more information on your company's background?
Puoi fornirci maggiori informazioni sullo sfondo della tua azienda?
(PWO-i for-NIR-tsi MAD-djo-ri in-for-ma-tsjo-ni sul-lo SFON-do del-la TU-a a-TSI-en-da?)

Let's talk about the timeline for this project.
Parliamo del cronoprogramma per questo progetto.
(PAR-lja-mo del KRO-no-pro-GRAM-ma per KWE-sto PRO-get-to.)

What are the key performance indicators for this collaboration?
Quali sono i principali indicatori di performance per questa collaborazione?
(KWA-li SO-no i prin-tsi-PA-li in-di-KA-to-ri di per-for-MAN-tsa per KWE-sta kol-la-bo-ra-tsjo-NE?)

Can we discuss the budget for this initiative?
Possiamo discutere il budget per questa iniziativa?
(POS-sja-mo dis-KU-te-re il BUD-get per KWE-sta i-ni-zja-TI-va?)

What are the risks involved in this partnership?
Quali sono i rischi coinvolti in questa partnership?
(KWA-li SO-no i RIS-ki ko-in-VOL-ti in KWE-sta part-ner-SHIP?)

How can we mitigate those risks?
Come possiamo mitigare quei rischi?
(KO-me POS-sja-mo mi-ti-GA-re kwei RIS-ki?)

Can we explore alternative solutions to this problem?
Possiamo esplorare soluzioni alternative a questo problema?
(POS-sja-mo es-plo-RA-re so-lut-tsjo-NI al-ter-NA-ti-ve a KWE-sto pro-BLE-ma?)

Let's discuss the scope of this project.
Parliamo dello scopo di questo progetto.
(PAR-lja-mo DEL-lo SKO-po di KWE-sto pro-GET-to.)

Can you provide us with a breakdown of the costs?
Puoi fornirci una scomposizione dei costi?
(PWO-i for-NIR-tsi U-na skom-po-SI-tsi-o-ne dei KOS-ti?)

Let's discuss the terms and conditions of the agreement.
Parliamo dei termini e delle condizioni dell'accordo.
(PAR-lja-mo dei TER-mi e DEL-le kon-di-TSJO-ni del-lak-KOR-do.)

What are the deliverables for this project?
Quali sono i deliverable per questo progetto?
(KWA-li SO-no i de-li-VE-ra-bil per KWE-sto pro-GET-to?)

Let's review the milestones for this initiative.
Rivediamo le pietre miliari per questa iniziativa.
(RI-ve-DJA-mo le PIET-re mi-LIA-ri per KWE-sta i-ni-za-TI-va.)

What are the payment terms for this deal?
Quali sono i termini di pagamento per questo affare?
(KWA-li SO-no i TER-mi di pa-GA-men-to per KWE-sto af-FA-re?)

Can you provide us with a timeline for the project?
Puoi fornirci un cronoprogramma per il progetto?
(PWO-i for-NIR-tsi un KRO-no-pro-GRAM-ma per il pro-GET-to?)

Let's talk about the quality standards for this partnership.
Parliamo degli standard di qualità per questa partnership.
(PAR-lja-mo del-LI stan-DARD di kwa-LI-ta per KWE-sta part-ner-SHIP?)

Can we discuss the role of each party in this deal?
Possiamo discutere il ruolo di ogni parte in questo affare?
(POS-sja-mo dis-KU-te-re il RUO-lo di ON-ni PAR-te in KWE-sto af-FA-re?)

How can we measure the success of this collaboration?
Come possiamo misurare il successo di questa collaborazione?
(KO-me POS-sja-mo mi-su-RA-re il suk-KES-so di KWE-sta kol-la-bo-ra-tsjo-NE?)

Let's discuss the legal implications of this agreement.
Parliamo delle implicazioni legali di questo accordo.
(PAR-lja-mo DEL-le im-pli-KA-tsi-o-ni LE-ga-li di KWE-sto ak-KOR-do.)

Can you provide us with a proposal for the project?
Puoi fornirci una proposta per il progetto?
(PWO-i for-NIR-tsi U-na pro-PO-sta per il pro-GET-to?)

Let's talk about the communication channels for this partnership.
Parliamo dei canali di comunicazione per questa partnership.
(PAR-lja-mo dei ka-NA-li di ko-mu-ni-ka-TSJO-ne per KWE-sta part-ner-SHIP?)

What are the expected outcomes of this collaboration?
Quali sono i risultati attesi di questa collaborazione?
(KWA-li SO-no i ri-ZUL-ta-ti at-TE-si di KWE-sta kol-la-bo-ra-tsjo-NE?)

Can we discuss the intellectual property rights involved in this deal?
Possiamo discutere i diritti di proprietà intellettuale coinvolti in questo affare?
(POS-sja-mo di-SKU-te-re i DIR-it-ti di pro-pri-e-tà in-tel-let-tua-le koi-nvol-ti in KWE-sto af-FA-re?)

Let's review the scope of work for this project.
Rivediamo la portata del lavoro per questo progetto.
(RI-ve-DJA-mo la por-TA-ta del LA-vo-ro per KWE-sto pro-GET-to.)

What are the key performance indicators for this initiative?
Quali sono gli indicatori chiave di performance per questa iniziativa?
(KWA-li SO-no gli in-DI-ka-to-ri KJA-ve di per-for-MAN-tsa per KWE-sta i-ni-za-TI-va?)

Can you provide us with a progress report for the project?
Puoi fornirci una relazione sullo stato di avanzamento del progetto?
(PWO-i for-NIR-tsi U-na re-la-TSJO-ne sul-lo STA-to di a-van-za-MEN-to del pro-GET-to?)

Let's talk about the potential risks and challenges for this partnership.
Parliamo dei potenziali rischi e sfide per questa partnership.
(PAR-lja-mo DEI po-ten-zja-LI RIS-ki e SFI-de per KWE-sta part-ner-SHIP?)

What are the technical requirements for this project?
Quali sono i requisiti tecnici per questo progetto?
(KWA-li SO-no i re-qui-SI-ti tek-NI-tsi per KWE-sto pro-GET-to?)

Can we discuss the marketing strategy for this initiative?
Possiamo discutere la strategia di marketing per questa iniziativa?
(POS-sja-mo di-SKU-te-re la stra-TE-gja di mar-KE-ting per KWE-sta i-ni-za-TI-va?)

Let's review the budget for this project.
Rivediamo il budget per questo progetto.
(RI-ve-DJA-mo il BUD-get per KWE-sto pro-GET-to.)

What are the expectations for the timeline of this project?
Quali sono le aspettative per il cronoprogramma di questo progetto?
(KWA-li SO-no le as-pet-TA-ti-ve per il KRO-no-pro-GRAM-ma di KWE-sto pro-GET-to?)

Can you provide us with a sample of your work?
Puoi fornirci un campione del tuo lavoro?
(PWO-i for-NIR-tsi un kam-PI-o-ne del TU-o la-VO-ro?)

Let's talk about the long-term goals for this partnership.
Parliamo degli obiettivi a lungo termine per questa partnership.
(PAR-lja-mo DEGLI o-bjet-TI-vi a LUN-go TER-mi-ne per KWE-sta part-ner-SHIP?)

What is the expected duration of this project?
Qual è la durata prevista di questo progetto?
(KWA-le LA du-RA-ta pre-VIS-ta di KWE-sto pro-GET-to?)

Can we discuss the terms for terminating this agreement?
Possiamo discutere i termini per la risoluzione di questo accordo?
(POS-sja-mo di-SKU-te-re i TER-mi-ni per la ri-sol-U-zjo-ne di KWE-sto ac-COR-do?)

What are the payment terms for this project?
Quali sono i termini di pagamento per questo progetto?
(KWA-li SO-no i TER-mi-ni di pa-GA-men-to per KWE-sto pro-GET-to?)

EXPRESSING GRATITUDE AND APOLOGIES

Thank you!
Grazie!
(GRA-tsee-eh)

I appreciate it.
Lo apprezzo.
(loh ah-PRET-tso)

I'm grateful for your help.
Sono grato per il tuo aiuto.
(SOH-noh GRAH-toh pehr eel TOO-oh ah-YOU-toh)

That was very kind of you.
È stato molto gentile da parte tua.
(eh STAH-toh MOHL-toh JEN-tee-leh dah PAR-teh TOO-ah)

Thank you so much!
Grazie mille!
(GRA-tsee-eh MEE-leh)

You're amazing!
Sei fantastico!
(sey fahn-TAH-stee-koh)

You really made my day.
Hai davvero reso la mia giornata.
(eye dahv-VEH-roh REH-zoh lah MEE-ah jor-NAH-tah)

I can't thank you enough.
Non posso ringraziarti abbastanza.
(nohn POH-soh reeng-RAHTS-yar-tee ah-bbas-TSAHN-za)

I'm so lucky to have you.
Sono così fortunato ad averti.
(SOH-noh KAH-tsee fohr-too-NAH-toh ahd ah-VEHR-tee)

I'm truly grateful.
Sono veramente grato.
(SOH-noh veh-rah-MEHN-teh GRAH-toh)

You have my heartfelt thanks.
Hai il mio sincero ringraziamento.
(eye eel MEE-oh seen-TSEH-roh reeng-RAHTS-yah-MEN-toh)

Thank you from the bottom of my heart.
Ti ringrazio dal profondo del cuore.
(tee reeng-RAHTS-yoh dahl proh-FOHN-doh del KWOH-reh)

I owe you one.
Ti devo una.
(tee DEH-vo oh-na)

You're a lifesaver.
Sei un salvatore.
(sey oon sahl-vah-TOH-reh)

You're the best!
Sei il migliore!
(sey eel meel-YOH-reh)

Your generosity means a lot to me.
La tua generosità significa molto per me.
(lah TOO-ah jeh-neh-roh-ZEE-tah see-NYEE-fee-kah MOHL-toh pehr meh)

I'm indebted to you.
Sono in debito con te.
(SOH-noh een DEH-bee-toh kohn teh)

I'm so grateful for your support.
Sono così grato per il tuo sostegno.
(SOH-noh KAH-tsee GRAH-toh pehr eel TOO-oh soh-STEH-nyoh)

You're a true friend.
Sei un vero amico.
(sey oon VEH-roh ah-MEE-koh)

You're a gem!
Sei una perla!
(sey OO-nah PEHR-lah)

I'm sorry.
Mi dispiace.
(mee dees-PYAH-cheh)

I apologize.
Mi scuso.
(mee SKOO-soh)

Please forgive me.
Per favore,perdonami.
(pehr fah-VOH-reh pehr-doh-NAH-mee)

I regret what I did/said.
Mi pento di quello che ho fatto/detto.
(mee PEHN-toh dee KWEHL-loh keh oh FAHT-toh/DEHT-toh)

I'm so sorry for the inconvenience.
Mi dispiace molto per l'inconveniente.
(mee dees-PYAH-cheh MOHL-toh pehr leen-kohn-veh-NYEN-teh)

My apologies for the mistake.
Le mie scuse per l'errore.
(leh MEE-eh SKOO-zeh pehr LEH-rroh-reh)

I take full responsibility.
Prendo piena responsabilità.
(PREN-doh pyeh-nah reh-sohn-see-bee-LY-tah)

I shouldn't have done/said that.
Non avrei dovuto fare/dire quello.
(nohn ah-VREH-ee doh-VOH-toh FAH-reh/DEE-reh KWEHL-loh)

181

Please accept my apologies.
Ti prego di accettare le mie scuse.
(tee PREH-goh dee ah-cheh-TAH-reh leh MEE-eh SKOO-zeh)

I'm sorry for any harm I caused.
Mi dispiace per eventuali danni causati.
(mee dees-PYAH-cheh pehr eh-ven-TWAA-lee DAHN-nee kahw-ZAH-tee)

I realize I was wrong.
Mi rendo conto di essere stato sbagliato.
(mee REHN-doh KOHN-toh dee eh-SEH-reh STAH-toh sbah-LYA-toh)

I'm sorry for my behavior.
Mi scuso per il mio comportamento.
(mee SKOO-soh pehr eel MEE-oh kohm-por-tah-MEN-toh)

That was uncalled for, and I'm sorry.
Non era giusto, e mi dispiace.
(nohn EH-rah JYOO-stoh, eh mee dees-PYAH-cheh)

I hope you can forgive me.
Spero che tu possa perdonarmi.
(SPEH-roh keh too POHS-sah pehr-doh-NAR-mee)

I'm sorry for letting you down.
Mi dispiace per averti deluso.
(mee dees-PYAH-cheh pehr ah-VEHR-tee deh-LOO-soh)

I'm sorry for not being there.
Mi dispiace non esserci stato.
(mee dees-PYAH-cheh nohn EH-ser-chee STAH-toh)

I feel terrible about what happened.
Mi sento terribilmente per quanto è accaduto.
(mee SEHN-toh teh-ree-bee-LY-men-teh pehr KWOHN-toh eh ahk-KAH-doo-toh)

Please don't be upset with me.
Per favore, non essere arrabbiato con me.
(pehr fah-VOH-reh, nohn EH-seh-reh ahr-rah-BYA-toh kohn meh)

I know I messed up, and I'm sorry.
So di aver combinato un guaio, e mi dispiace.
(soh dee ah-VEHR kohm-bee-NAH-toh oon GWAH-yoh, eh mee dees-PYAH-cheh)

I apologize for my mistake.
Chiedo scusa per il mio errore.
(KYEH-doh SKOO-zah pehr eel MEE-oh EH-rroh-reh)

GIVING AND RECEIVING COMPLIMENTS

You look amazing!
Sei stupendo/a!
(say stoo-PEN-doh/ah)

You did an excellent job!
Hai fatto un ot-ti-mo lavoro!
(say eye FAH-toh oht-TEE-moh la-VO-ro)

That outfit really suits you.
Quell'abbigliamento ti sta bene.
(say kwel-ahb-bee-LYAH-men-toh tee stah BEH-neh)

Your smile is beautiful.
Il tuo sorriso è bellissimo!
(say eel TOO-oh sor-REE-soh eh bel-LEE-see-moh)

You have a great sense of style.
Hai uno stilo eccezionale!
(say eye OO-no stee-LOH et-cheh-TSEE-oh-NAH-leh)

Your hair looks great today.
Oggi i tuoi capelli sono fantastici!
(say OH-jee ee TOO-oy kah-PEHL-lee SOH-noh fahn-TAH-stee-chee)

Your work is impressive.
Il tuo lavoro è imponente!
(say eel TOO-oh la-VO-ro eh eem-poh-NEN-teh)

You have a fantastic personality.
Hai una personalità fan-tastica!
(say eye OO-nah per-soh-na-lee-TAH fahn-TAH-stee-kah)

You have a wonderful voice.
Hai una voce stupenda!
(say eye OO-nah VOH-cheh stoo-PEN-dah)

You are such a talented artist.
Sei un artista molto talentuoso!
(say say oon ar-tee-stah MOHL-toh ta-len-TWOH-zoh)

You always make me laugh.
Mi fai sempre ridere.
(say mee fai SEM-preh ree-DEH-reh)

You have a brilliant mind.
Hai una mente brillante!
(say eye OO-nah MEN-teh bree-LAHN-teh)

You are a natural leader.
Sei un leader naturale!
(say say oon leh-AH-der nah-too-RAH-leh)

Your cooking is delicious.
La tua cucina è deliziosa!
(say lah TOO-ah koo-CHEE-nah eh deh-lee-TSEE-oh-sah)

You have a great eye for detail.
Hai un occhio per il dettaglio eccezionale!
(say eye oon OH-kyoh pehr eel deht-TA-lyoh et-cheh-TSEE-oh-NAH-leh)

You have a beautiful home.
La tua casa è bellissima!
(say lah TOO-ah KAH-sah eh bel-LEE-see-mah)

You are a great listener.
Sei un ascolta-tore eccezionale!
(say say oon askohl-TAH-toh-reh et-cheh-TSEE-oh-NAH-leh)

You are a true inspiration.
Sei una vera ispirazlone!
(say say OO-nah veh-rah ee-spee-rah-TSYOH-neh)

Your kindness is appreciated.
La tua gentilezza è molto apprezzata!
(say lahTOO-ah jen-tee-LEHT-tsah eh MOHL-toh ap-preh-TSAH-tah)

You have a great work ethic.
Hai una grande etica lavorativa.
(say eye OO-nah GRAHN-deh ehtee-KAH la-vo-REE-tiv-ah)

Thank you so much!
Grazie mille!
(say GRAH-tsyeh MEE-leh!)

That's very kind of you to say.
È molto gentile da parte tua dirlo.
(say eh MOHL-toh jen-TEE-leh dah PAR-teh TOO-ah DEER-loh)

I really appreciate it.
Lo apprezzo molto.
(say loh ap-PREHT-tsoh MOHL-toh)

You made my day!
Mi hai reso la giornata!
(say mee eye REH-soh lah jor-NAH-tah!)

That means a lot to me.
Significa molto per me.
(say see-nee-FEE-kah MOHL-toh pehr meh)

I'm flattered, thank you.
Sono lusingato/a, grazie.
(say SOH-noh loo-SEEN-gah-toh/ah, GRAH-tsyeh)

You're too kind.
Sei troppo gentile.
(say say TROH-poh jen-TEE-leh)

I'm glad you think so.
Sono contento/a che tu lo pensi.
(say SOH-noh kon-TEN-toh/ah keh too loh PEN-see)

That's really nice of you.
È davvero carino/a da parte tua.
(say eh dahv-VEH-roh kah-REE-noh/ah dah PAR-teh TOO-ah)

You're making me blush!
Mi fai arrossire!
(say mee fai ah-rroh-SEE-reh!)

I'm honored.
Sono onorato/a.
(say SOH-noh oh-noh-RAH-toh/ah)

That's very generous of you.
È molto generoso/a da parte tua.
(say eh MOHL-toh jeh-neh-ROH-soh/ah dah PAR-teh TOO-ah)

Thank you for saying that.
Grazie per averlo detto.
(say GRAH-tsyeh pehr ah-VEHR-loh DEHT-toh)

You have made my week!
Hai reso la mia settimana!
(say eye REH-soh lah MEE-ah seht-tee-MAH-nah!)

I'm really grateful.
Sono veramente grato/a.
(say SOH-noh veh-rah-MEHN-teh GRAH-toh/ah)

You're too sweet.
Sei troppo dolce.
(say say TROH-poh DOHL-cheh)

You're too kind to me.
Sei troppo gentile con me.
(say say TROH-poh jen-TEE-leh kohn meh)

I'm so happy to hear that.
Sono così felice di sentirlo/a.
(say SOH-noh KAH-zee feh-LEE-tcheh dee see-EHN-tir-loh/ah)

187

That's very thoughtful of you.

È molto premuroso/a da parte tua.

(say eh MOHL-toh preh-moo-ROH-soh/ah dah PAR-teh TOO-ah)

You've made my day/week/month/year!

Mi hai fatto la giornata/settimana/mese/anno!

*(say mee eye FAH-toh lah
jor-NAH-tah/seht-tee-MAH-nah/MEH-zeh/AHN-noh!)*

MAKING PHONE CALLS

Hello?
Ciao?
(chow)

Hi, this is [your name] speaking.
Ciao, sono [tuo nome] al telefono.
(chow, SOH-noh [two NOH-meh] al teh-LEH-foh-noh)

May I speak with [person's name], please?
Posso parlare con [nome della persona], per favore?
*(POH-soh pahr-LAH-reh kohn [NOH-meh DEHL-lah peh-RHOH-nah],
pehr fah-VOH-reh)*

Is [person's name] available?
[Nome della persona] è disponibile?
([NOH-meh DEHL-lah peh-RHOH-nah] eh dees-poh-NEE-bee-leh?)

Can you put me through to [person's name], please?
Puoi mettermi in contatto con [nome della persona], per favore?
*(PWAW-ee meht-TEHR-mee een kohn-TAHK-toh kohn [NOH-meh
DEHL-lah peh-RHOH-nah], pehr fah-VOH-reh)*

Could I speak to someone in charge, please?
Potrei parlare con qualcuno responsabile, per favore?
*(poh-TRAY pahr-LAH-reh kohn KWAHL-koo-noh rehs-pohn-SEE-beh-leh,
pehr fah-VOH-reh?)*

I'm sorry, I think I have the wrong number.
Mi dispiace, credo di aver sbagliato numero.
*(mee dee-SPYAH-cheh, KREH-doh dee ah-VEHR sbah-LYAH-toh
NOO-meh-roh)*

Who am I speaking with, please?
Scusi, con chi sto parlando?
(SKOO-zee, kohn kee stoh pahr-LAHN-doh?)

How are you today?
Come stai oggi?
(KOH-meh STY OH-jee?)

Good morning/afternoon/evening.
Buongiorno/pomeriggio/sera.
(BWOHN-johr-noh/poh-meh-REE-joh/SEH-rah)

I'm calling to [reason for call].
Sto chiamando per [motivo della chiamata].
(stoh kee-ah-MAN-doh pehr [moh-TEE-voh DEHL-lah kee-AH-mah-tah])

I'm returning your call.
Le sto richiamando.
(leh stoh ree-kyah-MAHN-doh)

I'm just following up on [previous conversation/topic].
Sto solo seguendo quanto abbiamo discusso riguardo [conversazione
precedente/argomento].
*(stoh SOH-loh seh-GWEN-doh KWAN-toh ahb-BYAH-moh
dee-SKOOH-soh ree-GWAR-doh [ ])*

Do you have a few minutes to speak?
Ha qualche minuto per parlare?
(ah KWAHL-keh mee-NOO-toh pehr pahr-LAH-reh?)

Can you hold on for a moment, please?
Puoi aspettare un momento, per favore?
(PWAW-ee ahs-peh-TAH-reh oon moh-MEN-toh, pehr fah-VOH-reh?)

I'll be with you in a moment.
Ci sarò tra un momento.
(chee sah-ROH trah oon moh-MEN-toh)

Thank you for holding.
Grazie per aver aspettato.
(GRAH-tsee-eh pehr ah-VEHR ahs-peh-TAH-toh)

I'm sorry, but [reason for decline].
Mi dispiace, ma [motivo del rifiuto].
(mee dee-SPYAH-cheh, mah [moh-TEE-voh del ree-FYOO-toh])

Can you repeat that, please?
Puoi ripetere, per favore?
(PWAW-ee ree-peh-TEH-reh, pehr fah-VOH-reh?)

I didn't catch that.
Non ho capito.
(nohn oh kah-PEE-toh)

Could you speak more slowly, please?
Potresti parlare più lentamente, per favore?
(poh-TREHS-tee pahr-LAH-reh pihoo len-TAH-men-teh, pehr fah-VOH-reh?)

Could you spell that, please?
Potresti ripetere la parola per lettera, per favore?
(poh-TREHS-tee ree-peh-TEH-reh lah pah-ROH-lah pehr let-TEH-rah, pehr fah-VOH-reh?)

I'll call back later.
Richiamerò più tardi.
(ree-kyah-MEH-roh pihoo TAR-dee)

Can you give me your phone number, please?
Puoi darmi il tuo numero di telefono, per favore?
(PWAW-ee DAHR-mee eel TOO-oh NOO-meh-roh dee teh-LEH-foh-noh, pehr fah-VOH-reh?)

Can you give me your email address, please?
Puoi darmi il tuo indirizzo email, per favore?
(PWAW-ee DAHR-mee eel TOO-oh een-DEE-ree-tsoh ee-MAYL, pehr fah-VOH-reh?)

I'll send you an email with the details.
Ti invierò un'email con i dettagli.
(tee een-VYEH-roh oon eh-MAYL kohn ee deh-TAH-lyee)

When would be a good time to call you back?
Quando sarebbe un buon momento per richiamarti?
(KWAN-doh sah-REH-beh oon bwohn moh-MEN-toh pehr
ree-kyah-MAR-tee?)

I'll make sure to call you back by [date/time].
Mi assicurerò di richiamarti entro il [data/ora].
(mee ah-see-koo-REH-roh dee ree-kyah-MAR-tee EHN-troh eel
[DAH-tah/OH-rah])

It was nice talking to you.
È stato bello parlare con te.
(eh STAH-toh BEHL-loh pahr-LAH-reh kohn teh)

Have a good day!
Buona giornata!
(BWOH-nah joor-NAH-tah)

Goodbye!
Arrivederci!
(ahr-ree-veh-DEHR-chee)

Hello, this is [your name] calling.
Buongiorno, sono [il tuo nome] che chiama.
(BWOHN-JOR-noh, SOH-noh [eel TOO-oh NOH-meh] kee KHA-mah)

May I speak with [person's name], please?
Posso parlare con [nome della persona], per favore?
(POHS-soh pahr-LAH-reh kohn [NOH-meh dehl-lah pehr-SOH-nah], pehr
fah-VOH-reh?)

I'm returning your call.
Sto richiamando la tua chiamata.
(stoh ree-kyah-MAHN-doh lah TOO-ah kee-AH-mah-tah)

I'm calling about [reason for call].
Sto chiamando riguardo a [ ].
(stoh kee-AH-mahn-doh ree-GWAHR-doh ah [ ])

Could you please transfer me to [department/person]?
Potresti per favore trasferirmi a [reparto/persona]?
(poh-TREHS-tee pehr fah-VOH-reh trahs-feh-REER-mee ah reh-PAHR-toh/pehr-SOH-nah]?)

I'm sorry, I think you have the wrong number.
Mi dispiace, penso che hai il numero sbagliato.
(mee dee-SPYAH-cheh, PEHN-soh keh ah-ee eel NOO-meh-roh sbah-LYAH-toh)

This is a reminder for [event/meeting].
Questo è un promemoria per [evento/riunione].
(KWES-toh eh oon proh-meh-MOH-ryah pehr eh-VEHN-toh/ree-oo-NYO-neh])

I'll call you back later.
Ti richiamo più tardi.
(tee ree-KYA-moh pihoo TAR-dee)

Can you please leave a message?
Puoi per favore lasciare un messaggio?
(PWOY pehr fah-VOH-reh lah-SYA-reh oon meh-SAH-joh?)

DESCRIBING FEELINGS AND EMOTIONS

I feel happy
Mi sento felice
(mee SEN-toh feh-LEE-cheh)

I am overjoyed
Sono ecstatico
(SOH-noh ek-STA-tee-koh)

I feel ecstatic
Mi sento ecstatico
(mee SEN-toh ek-STA-tee-koh)

I am delighted
Sono contento
(SOH-noh kon-TEN-toh)

I feel content
Mi sento contento
(mee SEN-toh kon-TEN-toh)

I am at peace
Sono in pace
(SOH-noh een PA-cheh)

I feel satisfied
Mi sento soddisfatto
(mee SEN-toh sod-dis-FAHT-toh)

I am pleased
Sono soddisfatto
(SOH-noh sod-dis-FAHT-toh)

I feel grateful
Sono grato
(SOH-noh GRAH-toh)

I am thankful
Sono grato
(SOH-noh GRAH-toh)

I feel blessed
Mi sento benedetto
(mee SEN-toh beh-neh-DET-toh)

I am elated
Sono felicissimo
(SOH-noh feh-lee-CHEE-see-moh)

I feel excited
Mi sento emozionato
(mee SEN-toh eh-moh-tzee-oh-NAH-toh)

I am enthusiastic
Sono entusiasto
(SOH-noh en-too-zyah-STOH)

I feel thrilled
Mi sento elettrizzato
(mee SEN-toh eh-leh-tree-TSAH-toh)

I am pumped
Sono eccitato
(SOH-noh ek-chee-TAH-toh)

I feel inspired
Mi sento ispirato
(mee SEN-toh is-pee-RAH-toh)

I am motivated
Sono motivato
(SOH-noh moh-tee-VAH-toh)

I feel empowered
Mi sento potenziato
(mee SEN-toh po-ten-tsyah-TOH-toh)

I am confident
Sono convinto
(SOH-noh kon-VEEN-toh)

I feel proud
Mi sento orgoglioso
(mee SEN-toh or-gohl-YOH-soh)

I am triumphant
Sono trionfatore
(SOH-noh tree-ohn-fah-TOH-reh)

I feel accomplished
Mi sento realizzato
(mee SEN-toh ree-ah-lee-TSAH-toh)

I am fulfilled
Sono appagato
(SOH-noh ap-pah-GAH-toh)

I feel joyful
Mi sento gioioso
(mee SEN-toh jo-YOH-soh)

I am euphoric
Sono euforico
(SOH-noh yoo-FOH-ree-koh)

I feel optimistic
Mi sento ottimista
(mee SEN-toh oht-tee-MEE-stah)

I am hopeful
Sono speranzoso
(SOH-noh speh-rahn-TSOH-soh)

I am relaxed
Sono rilassato
(SOH-noh ree-lahs-SAH-toh)

I feel calm
Mi sento calmo
(mee SEN-toh KAHL-moh)

I am composed
Sono composto
(SOH-noh kom-POH-stoh)

I feel confident
Mi sento sicuro
(mee SEN-toh SEE-koo-roh)

I am self-assured
Sono sicuro di me
(SOH-noh SEE-koo-roh dee MEH)

I feel secure
Mi sento al sicuro
(mee SEN-toh ahl SEE-koo-roh)

I am safe
Sono al sicuro
(SOH-noh ahl SEE-koo-roh)

I feel loved
Mi sento amato
(mee SEN-toh ah-MAH-toh)

I am appreciated
Sono apprezzato
(SOH-noh ah-preh-TSAH-toh)

I feel respected
Mi sento rispettato
(mee SEN-toh ree-speht-TAH-toh)

I am valued
Sono valorizzato
(SOH-noh vah-lo-ree-TSAH-toh)

I feel lonely
Mi sento solo
(mee SEN-toh SOH-loh)

DISCUSSING HEALTH AND WELL-BEING

I feel like I'm in a good place mentally and emotionally.
Mi sento bene mentalmente ed emotivamente.
(mi SENTO BE-ne men-tal-MEN-te ed e-mo-ti-VA-men-te)

I've been practicing gratitude and focusing on the positives in my life.
Sto praticando la gratitudine e mi concentro sugli aspetti positivi della mia vita.
(sto pra-ti-can-do la gra-TI-tu-di-ne e mi con-CEN-tro su GLI as-PE-tti po-SI-ti-vi DEL-la mia Vita)

I've been seeking support and help when I need it.
Sto cercando supporto e aiuto quando ne ho bisogno.
(sto CER-can-do SUP-por-to e AIU-to quando ne HO bisog-NO)

I've been feeling more confident and self-assured lately.
Mi sento più sicuro/a di me stesso/a ultimamente.
(mi sen-to più si-CU-ro/a di ME STEs-so/a UL-ti-ma-MEN-te)

I've been working on improving my communication skills in my relationships.
Sto lavorando per migliorare le mie abilità comunicative nelle relazioni.
(sto la-vo-ran-do per MIGLI-o-ra-re le MIE abilità co-MU-ni-ca-ti-ve nelle re-LA-zio-ni)

I've been taking steps to address any negative patterns or habits in my life.
Sto facendo passi per affrontare eventuali schemi o abitudini negative nella mia vita.
(sto fa-CEN-do PAS-si per af-FRON-ta-re eve-n-tua-li SCHE-mi o ab-bi-tu-DI-ni ne-GA-ti-VE nella MIA Vita)

I'm feeling optimistic about my future and the direction my life is going in.
Sono ottimista riguardo al mio futuro e alla direzione che sta prendendo la mia vita.
(SONO ot-ti-MI-sta ri-GUAR-do al MIO fu-TU-ro e al-la di-RE-zio-ne che sta pren-DEN-do la mia Vita)

I feel content with where I am in life right now.
Mi sento soddisfatto/a della mia posizione nella vita in questo momento.
(mi sen-to so-DIS-fat-to/a DEL-la mia SITUA-zio-ne at-tua-le)

How are you feeling today?
Come ti sen-ti oggi?
(koh-meh tee SEHN-tee OH-jee)

Are you taking care of yourself?
Ti sta-i pren-do cura di te stes-so?
(tee STAH-ee PREN-doh KOO-rah dee TEH STES-soh)

Have you been getting enough sleep?
Dor-mi ti a-bas-san-za-te?
(DOHR-mee tee ah-bahs-SAHN-tzah-teh)

Have you been feeling stressed lately?
Sen-ti te-stres-sa-to ul-ti-ma-men-te?
(SEHN-tee teh-STREHS-sah-toh uhl-tee-MAH-men-teh)

Are you experiencing any pain or discomfort?
Hai do-lo-ri o dis-com-for-to?
(HAI DOH-loh-ree oh DEES-kom-FOHR-toh)

Have you been eating a healthy diet?
Se-gui una di-E-ta sa-na?
(seh-GWEE OO-nah dee-EH-tah sah-NAH)

Are you taking any medications?
Pren-di far-ma-ci?
(PREN-dee FAHR-mah-chee)

Have you had any illnesses recently?
Hai avu-to mal-at-tie re-cen-te-men-te?
(HAI ah-voo-toh mah-LAHT-tee-eh reh-CHEN-teh-MEN-teh)

Have you been feeling fatigued or run down?
Sen-ti af-fat-to o sta-nco?
(SEHN-tee ahf-FAH-toh oh STAHN-koh)

Are you taking any steps to manage your stress?
Stai prendendo dei prov-VE-di-men-ti per gestire lo stress?
(STAI pren-DEN-doh day proh-VVEE-dee-MEN-tee pehr jeh-STEER-eh loh STRESS)

Have you been feeling anxious or depressed?
Sen-ti an-sia o de-pri-mi-to?
(SEHN-tee AHN-see-ah oh deh-pree-MEE-toh)

Have you been getting regular dental check-ups?
Fai vi-si-te den-ti-sti-che re-go-lar-men-te?
(fah-ee vee-SEE-teh den-tee-STEE-keh reh-goh-LAHR-men-teh)

Are you taking any supplements or vitamins?
Pren-di in-te-gra-to-ri ali-men-ta-ri o vi-ta-mi-ne?
(PREN-dee een-teh-GRAH-toh-ree ah-lee-MEN-tah-ree oh vee-tah-MEE-neh)

Do you have any family history of health problems?
Hai an-te-ce-den-ti fa-mi-li-a-ri di pro-ble-mi di sa-lu-te?
(HAI ahn-teh-CHEH-den-tee fah-MEE-lee-AH-ree dee proh-BLEH-mee dee sah-LOO-teh)

Are you getting enough rest and sleep?
Rice-vi ab-bas-tan-za di ri-po-so e son-no?
(REE-cheh-vee ahb-bahs-TAHN-tsah dee REE-poh-soh eh SON-noh)

Are you drinking enough water?
Be-vi ab-bas-tan-za di ac-qua?
(BEH-vee ahb-bahs-TAHN-tsah dee AHK-kwah)

Have you been experiencing any muscle or joint pain?
Hai do-lo-ri mus-co-la-ri o ar-ti-co-la-ri?
(HAI doh-LOH-ree moo-SKOH-lah-ree oh ahr-tee-KOH-lah-ree)

Have you been getting enough physical exercise?
Fai es-ser-ci-zio fi-si-co ab-bas-tan-te?
(fah-ee ehss-ehr-CHEE-tsyoh fee-SEE-koh ahb-bahs-TAHN-teh)

Have you been getting regular check-ups with your doctor?
Fai vi-si-te me-di-che re-go-lar-men-te con il tuo dot-to-re?
(fah-ee vee-SEE-teh meh-dee-keh reh-goh-LAHR-men-teh kohn eel too-oh DOHT-toh-reh)

Are you getting enough nutrients in your diet?
Rice-vi ab-bas-tan-za di nu-tri-en-ti nel-la vo-stra die-ta?
(REE-cheh-vee ahb-bahs-TAHN-tsah dee noo-tree-ehn-tee nell-lah VOH-strah dee-EH-tah)

Have you been feeling stressed or anxious lately?
Vi siete sen-ti-ti stres-sa-ti o an-sio-si ul-ti-ma-men-te?
(vee SYEH-teh sehn-TEE-tee STREH-sah-tee oh ahn-see-OH-see ool-tee-MAH-men-teh)

DESCRIBING JOBS AND PROFESSIONS

I am a doctor.
Io sono un medico
(EE-yo SO-no oon ME-dee-ko)

My profession is teaching.
La mia professione è l'insegnamento
(La MEE-a pro-FESS-yoh-neh eh lin-SEN-ya-men-to)

I work as an accountant.
Lavoro come contabile
(La-VO-ro KO-meh kohn-TAH-bi-leh)

I am a software engineer.
Sono un ingegnere del software
(SO-no oon in-jen-YEH-re del so-FWA-re)

My job title is project manager.
Il mio titolo di lavoro è project manager
(Eel MEE-o TEE-to-loh dee la-VO-ro eh PRO-jekt MAN-a-jer)

I am a lawyer.
Sono un avvocato
(SO-no oon av-vo-KA-to)

I work in sales.
Lavoro nelle vendite
(La-VO-ro NE-le VEN-di-teh)

My profession is engineering.
La mia professione è l'ingegneria
(La MEE-a pro-FESS-yoh-neh eh lin-jen-YEH-ri-a)

I am a scientist.
Sono uno scienziato
(SO-no OO-no shen-TSYA-to)

I work as a chef.
Lavoro come chef
(La-VO-ro KO-meh chef)

I am an artist.
Sono un artista
(SO-no oon ar-TEE-sta)

My job title is graphic designer.
Il mio titolo di lavoro è graphic designer
(Eel MEE-o TEE-to-loh dee la-VO-ro eh GRA-feeck deh-ZAI-ner)

I am a nurse.
Sono un infermiere / un'infermiera
(SO-no oon in-fer-MYEH-reh / oon-een-fer-MYEH-rah)

I work in marketing.
Lavoro nel marketing
(La-VO-ro nel mar-KE-ting)

My profession is architecture.
La mia professione è l'architettura
(La MEE-a pro-FESS-yoh-neh eh lar-kee-TET-tu-ra)

I am a journalist.
Sono un giornalista
(SO-no oon jor-na-LEE-sta)

My job title is CEO.
Il mio titolo di lavoro è ceo
(Eel MEE-o TEE-to-loh dee la-VO-ro eh CEO)

I am a dentist.
Sono un dentista
(SO-no oon den-TIS-ta)

I work in human resources.
Lavoro nelle risorse umane
(La-VO-ro NE-le ri-SOR-see OO-ma-neh)

My profession is psychology.
La mia professione è la psicologia
(La MEE-a pro-FESS-yoh-neh eh la pee-ko-LO-ja)

I am a veterinarian.
Sono un veterinario / un' veterinaria
(SO-no oon veh-teh-ree-NA-ryoh / oon veh-teh-ree-NA-rya)

My job title is software developer.
Il mio titolo di lavoro è sviluppatore di software
(Eel MEE-o TEE-to-loh dee la-VO-ro eh svee-loo-PA-toh-reh dee so-FWA-re)

I am a police officer.
Sono un poliziotto / una poliziotta
(SO-no oon po-lee-TSYO-to / oo-na po-lee-TSYOH-ta)

I work in customer service.
Lavoro nel servizio clienti
(La-VO-ro nel ser-VEE-tsyo KLEE-en-tee)

My profession is social work.
La mia professione è il lavoro sociale
(La MEE-a pro-FESS-yoh-neh eh eel la-VO-ro so-SHA-leh)

I am a financial analyst.
Sono un analista finanziario
(SO-no oon ah-na-LEE-sta fi-nan-TSYA-ryo)

I work in advertising.
Lavoro nella pubblicità
(La-VO-ro NE-la pub-bli-CHEE-ta)

My job title is accountant.
Il mio titolo di lavoro è contabile
(Eel MEE-o TEE-to-loh dee la-VO-ro eh kohn-TAH-bi-leh)

I am a construction worker.
Sono un operaio edile
(SO-no oon oh-peh-RA-yo eh-DEE-leh)

I work in IT.
Lavoro nel settore it
(La-VO-ro nel set-TO-reh IT)

My profession is medicine.
La mia professione è la medicina
(La MEE-a pro-FESS-yoh-neh eh la meh-DEE-chee-na)

I am a firefighter.
Sono un pompiere
(SO-no oon pom-PYE-reh)

I work as a real estate agent.
Lavoro come agente immobiliare
(La-VO-ro KO-meh A-jen-teh im-mo-bee-LYA-reh)

My job title is marketing manager.
Il mio titolo di lavoro è responsabile marketing
(Eel MEE-o TEE-to-loh dee la-VO-ro eh re-spon-SAH-beh-leh mar-KE-ting)

I am a mechanic.
Sono un meccanico
(SO-no oon mek-ka-NEE-ko)

I work in hospitality.
Lavoro nell'ospitalità
(La-VO-ro nel-loh-spee-ta-LEE-ta)

My profession is education.
La mia professione è l'educazione
(La MEE-a pro-FESS-yoh-neh eh leh-doo-kah-TSYO-neh)

I am a plumber.
Sono un idraulico
(SO-no oon ee-dra-O-lee-ko)

I work as a flight attendant.
Lavoro come assistente di volo
(La-VO-ro KO-meh as-si-STEN-teh dee VO-lo)

My job is in the fashion industry.
Il mio lavoro è nell'industria della moda
(Eel MEE-o la-VO-ro eh nel-LIN-doo-stree-a del-la MO-da)

GIVING AND RECEIVING INSTRUCTIONS

Let me show you how to do it.
Lasciami mostrarti come farlo.
(lah-SHA-mee mo-STRA-tee KO-meh FAR-loh)

This is how you do it.
Ecco come si fa.
(EK-ko KO-meh see FAH)

Follow these steps.
Segui questi passi.
(SE-gwee KWES-tee PASS-ee)

Pay attention to this.
Presta attenzione a questo.
(PRES-tah at-TEN-zio-neh ah KWES-toh)

Start by...
Inizia con...
(EE-nee-za kon)

First, you need to...
Prima di tutto, devi...
(PREE-mah dee TOO-toh, DEH-vee)

Take a look at this.
Guarda questo.
(GOR-da KWES-toh)

Read the instructions carefully.
Leggi le istruzioni con attenzione.
(LEJ-gee lees-true-ZYO-nee kon at-TEN-zio-neh)

You need to be careful with...
Devi fare attenzione a...
(DEH-vee FAH-reh at-TEN-zio-neh ah)

Make sure you...
Assicurati che...
(AH-see-koo-RAH-tee keh)

Don't forget to...
Non dimenticare di...
(NON dee-men-TEE-kreh dee)

Keep in mind that...
Tieni presente che...
(TYEH-nee pre-ZEN-teh keh)

It's important that you...
È importante che tu...
(EH eem-por-TAHN-teh keh too)

I need you to...
Ho bisogno che tu...
(OH bee-ZO-nyo keh too)

Can you please...
Puoi per favore...
(POO-oy pehr fa-VO-reh)

Would you mind...
Ti dispiace...
(TEE dee-SPYA-cheh)

It would be great if you could...
Sarebbe fantastico se tu potessi...
(SA-reh-beh fahn-TAS-tee-ko seh too poh-TEH-si)

Please remember to...
Per favore, ricorda di...
(pehr fa-VO-reh, ree-KOR-da dee)

You have to...
Devi...
(DEH-vee)

Try to...
Cerca di...
(CHER-kah dee)

Okay, I understand.
Va bene, ho capito.
(VAH BEH-neh, oh kah-PEE-toh)

I see what you mean.
Capisco quello che intendi.
(kah-PEES-ko KWEL-lo keh een-TEN-dee)

That makes sense.
Ha senso.
(ah SEN-so)

All right, got it.
Va bene, ho capito.
(VAH BEH-neh, oh kah-PEE-toh)

Sure, I can do that.
Certo, posso farlo.
(CHER-toh, POH-soh FAR-loh)

No problem.
Nessun problema.
(ne-SSOON pro-BLE-ma)

Thanks for explaining that.
Grazie per avermelo spiegato.
(GRAH-tsee-eh pehr ah-ver-MEH-loh SPYEH-gah-toh)

I'll make a note of it.
Ne terrò nota.
(neh TEH-roh NO-tah)

I'll keep that in mind.
Me lo ricorderò.
(meh loh ree-KOR-deh-roh)

I'll do my best.
Farò del mio meglio.
(FAH-roh del MEE-oh ME-lyoh)

Please let me know if I have any questions.
Per favore, fammi sapere se ho domande.
(pehr fa-VO-reh, FAHM-mee sa-PEH-reh seh oh doh-MAN-deh)

Could you repeat that, please?
Potresti ripetere, per favore?
(poh-TRES-tee ree-peh-TEH-reh, pehr fa-VO-reh)

Could you clarify that for me?
Potresti chiarirmelo, per favore?
(poh-TRES-tee kee-ah-REER-meh-loh, pehr fa-VO-reh)

I'm not sure I understand. Can you explain it again?
Non sono sicuro di aver capito. Potresti spiegarmelo di nuovo?
(non SO-no see-KOO-roh dee ah-VER kah-PEE-toh. poh-TRES-tee SPYEH-gar-MEH-loh dee NOO-vo)

Sorry, I didn't catch that. Can you repeat it?
Scusa, non ho capito. Potresti ripetere?
(SKOO-sah, non oh kah-PEE-toh. poh-TRES-tee ree-peh-TEH-reh)

Would you mind showing me?
Ti dispiacerebbe mostrarmelo?
(tee dee-SPYA-cheh-REH-beh moh-STRA-meh-loh)

Can I ask a question?
Posso fare una domanda?
(POH-soh FAH-reh OO-nah doh-MAN-dah)

Can you break it down for me?
Potresti spezzare in parti per me?
(poh-TRES-tee SPETTS-sa-reh een PAR-tee pehr meh)

Can you give me an example?
Potresti darmi un esempio?
(poh-TRES-tee DAR-mee oon eh-SEM-pyo)

Let me show you how to do it.
Lascia che ti mostri come farlo.
(LAH-shah keh tee MO-stree KOH-meh FAR-loh)

Printed in Great Britain
by Amazon